Contemporary Exhibition-Making and Management

I0472881

This book provides a unique insight into contemporary curation and management in an innovative London-based gallery.

Using a critical in-depth case study exploration of IMT art gallery's 'successes' and 'failures', it illustrates and evaluates contemporary issues and challenges in curatorial initiatives and exhibition-making strategies. IMT operates as a 'hybrid space', combining characteristics of both the commercial gallery sector with non-profit artist-led or garage spaces while retaining affiliations to academic teaching and research. This book explores its structure, behaviour, history, partnerships, and exhibition programme through a variety of disciplinary lenses, bringing together cultural, creative, economic, and pedagogical perspectives, as well as the effect of recent sociocultural impacts of the global financial crisis, and the COVID-19 pandemic.

Research-based and thought-provoking, this study will be of great interest to researchers, advanced students and professionals in curatorial studies, museum and gallery management, and art markets.

Mark Rohtmaa-Jackson is a curator and Assistant Professor in Fine Art Critical Theory and Curatorial Practice at Northumbria University, UK.

Routledge Focus on the Global Creative Economy
Series Editor: Aleksandar Brkić, *Goldsmiths, University of London, UK*

This innovative Shortform book series aims to provoke and inspire new ways of thinking, new interpretations, emerging research, and insights from different fields. In rethinking the relationship of creative economies and societies beyond the traditional frameworks, the series is intentionally inclusive. Featuring diverse voices from around the world, books in the series bridge scholarship and practice across arts and cultural management, the creative industries and the global creative economy.

For more information about this series, please visit: www.routledge.com/Routledge-Focus-on-the-Global-Creative-Economy/book-series/RFGCE

Contemporary Exhibition-Making and Management

Curating IMT Gallery as a Hybrid Space

Mark Rohtmaa-Jackson

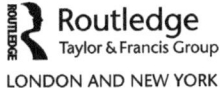
Routledge
Taylor & Francis Group

LONDON AND NEW YORK

First published 2023
by Routledge
4 Park Square, Milton Park, Abingdon, Oxon OX14 4RN

and by Routledge
605 Third Avenue, New York, NY 10158

Routledge is an imprint of the Taylor & Francis Group, an informa business

British Library Cataloguing-in-Publication Data
A catalogue record for this book is available from the British Library

ISBN: 978-1-032-05386-8 (hbk)
ISBN: 978-1-032-05528-2 (pbk)
ISBN: 978-1-003-19795-9 (ebk)

DOI: 10.4324/9781003197959

Typeset in Times New Roman
by Newgen Publishing UK

Contents

Acknowledgements and Thanks

For the gallery, I first and foremost thank Lindsay Friend, for her intensive dedication to IMT. I also thank all the many artists, curators, and technicians who helped the project exist and make interesting things happen, whose work with the gallery has been so crucial in its life, often made that much more powerful through their belief in IMT as an idea more than a building.

I am immensely grateful and indebted to everyone who sacrificed their time to talk to me specifically with the aim of writing this account: Ana Benlloch, Uma Breakdown, David Burrows, Kirsten Cooke, Charles Danby, Graham Dunning, Karl England, Pawel Kaminski, Vanessa Page, Maggie Roberts, Lotte Rose Kjær Skau, Andrew/Chong Boon Pok, Nicole Sansone Ruiz, Stuart Tait, NaoKo TakaHashi, and of course Lindsay Friend, but also to others over the years whose conversations have remained in my mind and made it into this text less explicitly. I'd also like to thank my colleagues and students at Northumbria who discussed, challenged, and inspired some themes that have made it into this book, and thank those who offered and gave their time, attention and expertise to read and comment on various drafts: Lindsay and Kirsten, Julie Crawshaw, Allan Hughes, Luke McCreadie, and Aleksandar Brkić. And Matthew Potter, whose advice is always invaluable and without whom this book wouldn't have made it beyond an idea.

Finally, this book is only a little thing, but it is for Monica and Kai, who are everything.

Introduction

Being a curator involved in the exhibition-making process is not the same as being a visitor to that exhibition. To work with art from a curatorial perspective is to become familiar with an artwork's construction, mechanisms, fragility, history, language, and relationship to its maker(s) and to learn of new relationships to audiences with an intimacy and intensity that goes beyond what is often expected of a casual visitor. Sometimes the work of a curator is about helping convey an artist's intentions. Sometimes it is to challenge that intention or detract from it to have a different conversation entirely (Barthes 1977).

Being the curator of an art gallery, especially one who was involved in a gallery's beginnings, is to carry that perspective through the organization itself. We step into it, speaking through its mouths, learning the feel of its viscera.[1] The gallery is a series of utterances, a hybrid of mouths, and this book tries to describe these mouths: their allure, their entanglements, their architecture, and contents. For this book, *the* gallery is a specific contemporary art gallery: IMT.

There are concessions I have made for the nature of a book like this. It contains some history, theory, and practice. However, these compartmentalizations are synthetic in terms of the messiness and porousness of IMT's organization. Many routes we plan or follow with IMT have been taken through crisis and hope, some out of the infringement of personal lives and the arguments of pride, others through apathy but more through love and joy, and this shifting set of impulses drives much more of the shape of

DOI: 10.4324/9781003197959-1

IMT's appearances in the world than the application of business criteria. This will show up in the text.

As a curator of IMT, I am entangled in the paratext of the gallery (of which this book is a part), and an actor within this text. This then is a hagiography, a performative account of IMT historicizing as it still lives. Therefore, this is a text dominated by my writing of it, but I've tried to maintain a degree of polyphony as much as possible though the significant input of other curators and artists involved in IMT. A large part of this polyphony is following the interpretations and associated interests of others in this decoding (perhaps also using 'decoding' in a Deleuzian sense). So the book leans towards projects in which I was involved, these are more *within reach* (Ahmed 2006), but this should not overshadow the significant contributions of others: Lindsay Friend, IMT's director, who has had a substantial input into IMT's curatorial direction; Kirsten Cooke, the gallery's curator from 2021 to 2022, the time of writing hence their particular influence; Nicole Sansone Ruiz, co-curator from 2014 to 2016; Pawel Kaminski, who regularly curated at the gallery between 2005 and 2012; Gordon Shrigley, curator of the Filmarmalade/Marmalade[2] programme, and the other invited curators and artists who each contributed their research and energies to the programme.

This is an IMT project in attitude, form, and function. Much of this book, including its structure, has been guided first and foremost by conversations with those involved in our work and, because of this, might subvert some formal expectations. Perhaps all IMT itself is a kind of conversation. As such there are overriding themes, yet also points at which ideas are left open for another day.

The hybridity of IMT is partly because we are imposters. We trained as artists not businesspeople or even curators, so there is an inconsistency in this work. Where this text veers furthest from academic writing and its expected conventions may be where it veers closest to how our work is communicated in real terms to those artists, audiences, curators, and partners who interact with it. So, mirroring the case study, this book is also a hybrid, and not a clean one. It is a hybrid of different styles of writing and research, sometimes scholarly, sometimes anecdotal, sometimes channelled through cultural studies, epistemology, autoethnography, epistolary. Oh, and it is often irrational. It is really a way of getting down a kind of cultural management practiced, like art often is, more through empiricism than through academic study. The hybrid breaks rules of business. It is a complexification, like the metamodelling of Guattari (1995:58, for example), because its thresholds are unclear. It crosses the human/alien threshold and makes a third thing. Therefore, the shape of this book may at times appear like the early stages of installing an exhibition or the point after which it has ended: artwork sitting alongside packing materials, a cat litter tray, a suitcase containing a week's worth of clothes, items waiting for storage and a bag waiting for the bins, notes and interviews gathering in folders, all in the aim of trying to effectively communicate a curatorial device, to see whether this work can be of use. I am surrounded by influences that internalize like accents. I take them into my language.

The gallery is both a physical operation and a project yet to be, so this book is a *coming after* whilst the gallery is a *making before*. If it is a research project, as I believe it is, then it is practice-based research and experimentalist in approach. We come as we are. Some of what this book does comes from being relatively well-read though not necessarily in the right field, at the right time or to the right depth. I have tried to produce here a hybrid of the expectations of academic writing and publishing and of the kind of 'wild and transversal writing' that Gerald Raunig laments in *Factories of Knowledge Industries of Creativity* (2013:35). I imagine successive drafts and revisions may have pulled this more to the former, but I hope there are still vibrations of the latter.

This account is more as a series of dynamic relations (as a diagram) than a coherent series of discrete objects. IMT is unsettled and in this way, in Guattari's terms, can be thought of as a system of transformation with exhibitions that are momentary. According to Guattari (as summarized in Watson 2009:12), diagrams are not representational but generative, and as such this is a generative account of IMT and may differ from expectations of representation. This is partly because IMT itself is generative rather than representational, and because getting close to IMT in its mode of becoming is the aim of this text. Therefore, there may be moments in which this text appears inexact. It may mislead theory and abridge ideas that were not designed to be connected. I am attempting a form of alchemy, of 'as above, so below'; to bring things together to show their underlying equivalence, to show that these things, at every intensity of their structure, are in some way the same. That this is the methodology is partly to deterritorialize, to see IMT as an assemblage (Deleuze and Guattari 1984), and partly because the gallery changes whilst we write and speak about it and is therefore only visible through intensities.

Lastly, there is also IMT's prerogative. There are projects for the gallery on the way, ideas and suggestions, desires and practicalities; working through plans we have on hold from the COVID-19 pandemic or whilst we identify avenues of funding or rewrite failed bids. There is always some uncertainty in how we should do some of these things; always some important conversations we are having about IMT's function that we need to address. We have been asked for descriptions of what we do whether, post-COVID, through an interest in how smaller, non-commercial spaces have adapted to unpredictable circumstances (Tomlinson 2021) or to map manifestos (IMT Gallery 2021) in an era in which cultural organizations are under renewed scrutiny.

As can be the case for art organizations that ceaselessly reach for the contemporary, IMT constantly reinvents itself, and its utterances are usually opportunistic for whatever it is becoming. This is the first attempt to trace intensities through its past, but we do so conscious that this is not a completed project, our search for hybridity continues to play out in our practice. This book then is an intervention into a practice that is a work in progress; a process of investigation; a not doing theory properly.

I am in Seyðisfjörður, Iceland, visiting the LungA School, an art school founded partly on anarchist values. And there, through the window of the hostel where I'm staying, the glacier moves down the fjord, so I'm told but can't see. It slips down and away, its slipping visible only in space not in time, like a vast candy imperceptibly yet deliberately licked into a sliver in the mouth of a god. I am writing this book for a candy. I am writing this book for a candy being sucked until it is gone.

Notes

1 Re: Burroughs 1985:48.
2 Publishers of artists films and critical theory.

1 Orientations

In *Friday 13th Part V: A New Beginning* (1985) the franchise's masked killer, Jason Voorhees, is only a copycat, Roy Burns, an ambulance driver driven to psychosis though seeing the mutilated body of his abandoned son. Burns is more used to putting bodies back together than ripping them apart. He involves himself in a ritual of death and healing, hidden from the audience by his ceremonial robes of killer and healer: dismembering bodies in one scene, collecting them in his ambulance in the next. The dichotomy is repeated: a motorist gets a distress flare in his mouth, a tool and an orifice both ordinarily deployed to attract help, here used as a means of silencing. Later, two teenagers are being watched by a peeping tom, but it is the teenagers whose eyes are obliterated. Even the very end of the film sees a reversal when the franchise's recurring hero, Tommy Jarvis, dons the mask of the killer.

In April 2013 at *Masquerade – Be Another*, a group exhibition at the Stephen Lawrence Gallery, London[1], Roy Burns is introduced as one of the avatars in the performance *All the Fantasies of the People* by the collaborative art practice Plastique Fantastique. In July 2013 Roy Burns reappeared in performances of the same name at Grand Union, Birmingham, and IMT Gallery, and then in August at the Wysing Art Centre, Cambridgeshire. *All the Fantasies of the People* was an artwork 'presented as the fiction of a community of non-community – a holding pattern of void points' (Burrows and O'Sullivan 2014:272).

In O'Sullivan and Burrows' textual 'metamodelling' of Plastique Fantastique they suggest that a function of this work, and of art more widely, can be thought of as 'non-schizoanalysis' via the

DOI: 10.4324/9781003197959-2

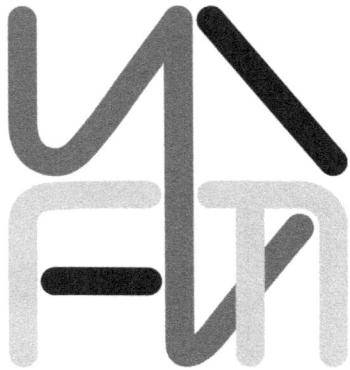

Figure 1.1 IMT Gallery logo/Sigil (2022), made by Plastique Fantastique.

'non-philosophy' of François Laruelle, a deployment of some of the tools of schizoanalysis towards ends outside of or beyond the project of Deleuze and Guattari. They propose 'not a human technology in this sense but something more alien' (ibid. 276). This desire to find another way of doing is, for the individual members of Plastique Fantastique,[2] a means of refusing some of the systems and structures of late capitalism and redeploying, hacking, or modding others. As someone asked to join Plastique Fantastique for this series of performances, I chose Roy Burns to be my avatar. He represented, for me, a vehicle through which I could attempt to be part of this 'community of non-community' through the identity that I had assumed and that had led me to be acquainted with Plastique Fantastique: that of a curator.

But let me be a subject before I am an object. Roy Burns is not only a character that comes out of IMT, but, in my own metamodelling, *is* IMT. I use these models: Roy Burns, five mouths, a Third Mind, a cult, a kraat, a television studio, as aids to help us invent, plan, manage, curate, and describe IMT. They are like servitors of chaos magic (Hine 1995) or, following O'Sullivan, diagrammatic re-engineerings, changing the past through the present to allow for different futures to emerge (O'Sullivan 2016:24).

We nest these servitors and then put them to use: Roy is the fourth of five mouths that form a diagram, a means of IMT holding two contrary positions, balancing two roles: a commercial–non-profit, online–offline, an artist–curator, a colleague–kin, an author–vessel, a killer–healer. A dialectic. A hybrid; always unsettled between repositions. An idea or a diagram floating in, or laid over, the symbolic order of the art world under capitalism. Burns is a Walk-in[3] jumping into the writing to execute esoteric actions as a monster out of the gallery's past. And he is here because he is my way of trying to find other forms of relations than those defined by the systemic abuses of the art world and its authority over most major forms of value and exchange. He is in a state of hyperarousal from work-related stress.

I write this text as it seems important to describe galleries like IMT in the frame of the rise of curating as an academic discipline. In much contemporary art discourse on curating, curatorial practice is often, although not always, a thing described as if orphaned from the material conditions of its practice. In the case of IMT

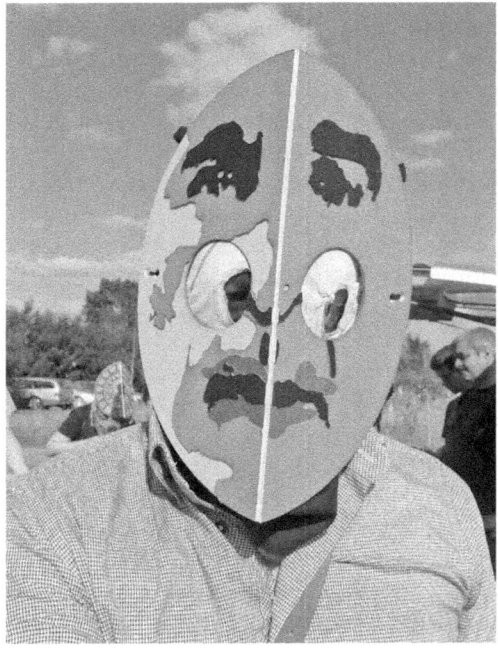

Figure 1.2 Roy Burns mask (version 2) at the *Space-Time: The Multiverse* music festival, Wysing Arts Centre, August 2013. Photograph by Mark Rohtmaa-Jackson, mask by Plastique Fantastique.

the very existence of a curatorial practice is so bound up with the material conditions of its emergence, and the privileges afforded by these conditions, so a discussion of these conditions is included.

IMT is a hybridization of practices, structures, and desires, and it is not a closed project but seeks other kinds of relations to study and understand them. IMT is nothing pure.[4] As such, it seems to me that a case study like this might be useful, if not answering questions about what we do, how and why we do it, then making space for the discussion of themes: death, dreams, improvisation, thresholds, holding, and collaborations. The case study that this book is concerned with was always meant to be a model to share, like a half-sucked sweet, and this book is one view of that model.

I was the founding curator of this model: a London-based art gallery variously known as IMT, Image Music Text, and IMT Gallery, a contemporary art gallery co-founded in 2005 in East London with the gallery's director Lindsay Friend. This book explores the ethos, working practices and sustainability of IMT, and its adaption through changes to the sector between 2005 and 2022. Ultimately, however, this is a book about curating. It comes from our experiences of studying art to be artists, and then finding ourselves working instead to help make exhibitions with others. In fact, this book is a curating. My work as a curator is often pattern recognition through onslaught of information (McLuhan 1964:VIII),[5] and, as a curating, this book is also pattern recognition. This is its formulation and is essential to understand its structure and limitations but also to understand how I come to the curatorial and my praxis against and within it.

I stepped into this space as an artist newly aware of how galleries and institutions monopolize the articulation of making. The art world as hegemonic and dominated by the marketization of creativity (Stalder and Sollfrank 2021:11) and that 'creative endeavour [is] defined as little more than the performance of institutions which claim to serve those ends' (Illich 1971:1). As we became more embedded in the spaces and structures of this monopoly, it becomes evident that we would need to pull our work in strange and illogical directions to retain our sense that we weren't complicit in the alienation of people to their making. So perhaps, like Burroughs (1985:18)[6] and like Chris Kraus (2018:90), this is me trying to write my way out.

My aim in this book is to decode what a practice-based curatorial project might be that fails to site itself within a specific type of institution. This is a decoding as part of the transformation of the subject: IMT, and to make something ~~useful~~.[7] I talk materially about immaterial structures and actions as well as denigrate these structures to be somehow lesser than the things they attach themselves to. As points of departure, I offer some parallels that are both conceptual and metaphorical. I use them as diagrams (in a post-Guattarian sense) to bring together different models in the hope of building new worlds. I use a tight network of relatively loose terms: unsettled, fugitive, and hybrid, to describe how a case study like this finds itself positioned within what can likewise be only loosely defined as an industry or, even more abstractly, as a world. I use the terminology of remaining 'unsettled' after Lucy Steeds' 'What is the Future of Exhibition Histories? Or, toward Art in Terms of Its Becoming-Public' (2016:17); 'fugitive' from the glossary of William Burroughs' *Junky* (1953),[8] and the 'hybrid' from the board game *Space Hulk* (Halliwell 1989), the domain of the fifth mouth, where it describes an alien–human amalgam. For in *Space Hulk*, the Imperium of Man has an imperial face, whereas the face of the hybrid revolves around the tongue. Therefore, I also talk about sweets (candies), aliens (extra-terrestrials), and mouths. This is not a philosophy but a practice, more a motif than a metanarrative. The writing of this book posits the hypothesis that it is only through the doing (the actual curating) that the space within which solutions might be negotiated can be found or as Richard Foreman puts it: 'Our art then [...] shows, concretizes, that which [...] stands under what is chosen, so that choice is alive and energized' (Forman in Lotringer 1978:125).

We have called IMT alternately a space, a gallery, a project, a company, even a business, but this story of IMT is very much from the perspective of it being a project, with all the emphases that suggests. For O'Doherty, projects describe 'short-term art made for specific sites and occasions'; a 'vernacular' impermanence that challenges the historical: a 'rumour' (1999:70). IMT's existence, partly through our own anxieties, always contained its death and, following this, its disappearance into rumour, and this impermanence is a defining characteristic of its unsettled state.

Despite arguing for the unsettled, it is worth, with a view to full disclosure, admitting other political and/or critical orientations, perhaps almost ideological ones, that may help make use of what follows. Think of 'orientation' in the meanings attached to it by Sara Ahmed (2006). This use of orientation is helpful in how it is an embodied relation to influences (especially to physical texts) whilst also being representative of a queer disorientation. Ahmed's deployment of orientation is also useful for its exposure of how some of the more problematic of these influences are here because they are *within reach*. In looking back on the work of IMT in the years since its founding, this amalgamation of wilful disorientation and co-opting of that which is within reach is a visible characteristic of the project. Perhaps this is a characteristic common to other organizations in the sector. Perhaps it is a characteristic born from the anxieties and pressures of keeping the project going.

And so two most relevant orientations are: the bid for absolute or wilful incompetence made by Deleuze and Guattari (1984:380–456 and 232–75, respectively); and an autonomy from causality and control made by William S. Burroughs across his oeuvre, which, for me, is more of a demand for agency, achieved through a decoding, subverting and reversing of the structures, instruments and practices of power. I hope to demonstrate that am not blind to the problems that these raise, although I was more blind to these in 2005 when IMT was founded than I am now. And whilst the identity and practice of the kinds of art worlds that IMT belongs to are inarguably a product of the white Western colonial imagination, it was, simultaneously, a vainglorious attempt (as many such galleries also seem to be) to attack, subvert, or replace this image. This incompetence was not wilful but may well be absolute. Its indifference to some urgent arguments perhaps irresponsible, and its lust for autonomy born from a particular breed of intellectual and cultural privilege. As such this is a critical case study that is also an autopsy, and hopefully its usefulness is in its evisceration being by its own bloodied hands. The autopsy is made easier because of IMT's attempts at transparency. Although it flies in darkness, the guts of the Penanggalan are entirely visible hanging beneath their mouths.

Notes

1 The Stephen Lawrence Gallery was founded following the 1999 Macpherson report, which made explicit the existence of institutional racism in the Metropolitan Police.
2 The consistent members of Plastique Fantastique are currently David Burrows, Alex Marzeta, Simon O'Sullivan, and Vanessa Page.
3 A Walk-in is a 'high-minded entity who is permitted to take over the body of another human being who wishes to depart. [...] The motivation for a Walk-in is humanitarian' (Montgomery 1979:13). It should be noted that the term Walk-in refers to both the entity and the body taken over.
4 Re: *Penda's Fen* (1974).
5 An explicit example is the exhibition *All I Can See Is Trees* (2023), designed around the confluence of a story David Burrows tells about a severed foot left in the aftermath of the 1991 Victoria Station bombing; the NFL concussion crisis leaving former Pittsburgh Steelers player 'Iron' Mike Webster with cracked feet held together with glue and duct tape; and a solitary Yeti foot from the partly missing Doctor Who story *The Abominable Snowmen* (1967), set in the mountains of Tibet. This pattern then becomes an investigation of other themes: especially around bodies and labour post-pandemic (Rohtmaa-Jackson 2023).
6 Obviously, capitalism and publicly shooting dead your partner when selling a gun are not the same things, but nor are they entirely unconnected.
7 I am using the strike-through here as *sous rature*, following Derrida's adoption of Heidegger's term.
8 'Not only do the words change meanings but the meanings vary locally at the same time. A final glossary, therefore, cannot be made of words whose intentions are fugitive' (Burroughs 2003:133).

2   The Cult of Possible Elements

In 2021 I invited Plastique Fantastique to come and speak via video conferencing at an event for a research group that went under the remit of Curatorial and Collaborative Practices. Live avatars[1] read tarots from a deck of cards called *Your Future in Foolish Memes* (2020). One of the avatars, Feveractal, was not present but spoke from a pre-recorded video. They spoke, forcibly, about collaboration:

> – a collaboration is experimental – it will take chances, test things out – it will involve a collaboration with the outside – yes – in fact, one cannot collaborate with the outside but only lure it in – which invariably means for yous, the result will be bloody – heads will be need to be put on the block – oh yes.
>
> (Feveractal 2021)

At IMT there are many residues of collaborations that function to build the gallery's myth. Each collaboration forms part of the world of IMT and is, in essence, a practice of the director, Friend, writing her own history. For myself I am a vessel or the Walk-in (Lewis 2001:368), soulless and wanting to be occupied by another, and each collaboration helps displace this absence.

We can identify an old curatorial urge: an effort to seek out what Fitzgerald calls, 'the compensations and refuges of life' (Fitzgerald 1926:1), and how we seem to locate these in the social joy bound up with the curatorial: talking, drinking, smoking, and being in love; private joy at art and thinking about or hoping for happiness, a desire of mouths. Any alleviation from depressions

DOI: 10.4324/9781003197959-3

and anxieties; an instrumentalization of a labour of love (Doussan 2013:3–5). There is also the drive to support artists in an art world in which 'art institutions, galleries, and funding bodies have failed the artists they supposedly serve' (Black Swan 2022b:322). As young artists we felt that a world we were promised was failing us and other artists around us, and IMT hoped to be different.

To try and describe IMT's approach I am going to discuss two projects at the gallery and do so with the help of some of the artists who made them: *AAS: The Cult of Possible Elements* (2014) and *This Is a Not-Me* (2020). Each reveals a heightened curator/artist dynamic that describes where IMT is and where it might be going. Although other exhibitions and events over the years haven't played out as explicitly as these, they all share some tendency from which this approach grew or some residue of it.

The Cult of Possible Elements arose from an offer to the art collective AAS to have free reign of IMT's exhibition space for a day. We knew some members of AAS from their role in Plastique Fantastique for *All the Fantasies of the People* (2013) at IMT as well as a version of the performance of *Cloud gives birth to new animal: Plastique Fantastique feedback loop to call forth neuropatheme (subject-without-experience a.k.a. fux-the-shadow, blanck-the-systemick-system-kcuf-dik, empty-the-cave, stone-blanko-the-scum, no-head-ass-ee-fal, etc.)* at IMT's stand in Art13.[2] AAS's practices overlapped with Plastique Fantastique, which both allowed for us to have a basic critical context for their interests in philosophy, as well as sympathy for their collaborative rituals and how they might be articulated to different audiences in a gallery context.

We'd mutually arranged a studio visit and were told about past projects, and the detail, complexity and, in some cases, arbitrariness of how they were designed and played out. The work was diagrammatic. Uma Breakdown describes how the work is not only generated from a diagram yet used the concept of diagrams to both think about and perform the work, as well as articulate its themes and its agency.[3] There were conversations around the possibility of an exhibition, but the idea then resolved into a performance. The performance comes together as a series of interests layered over one another:

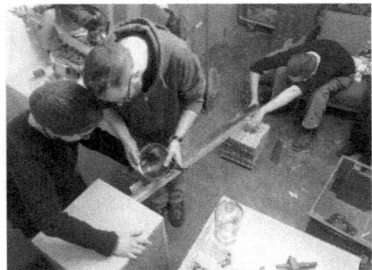

Figure 2.1 AAS in their studio developing the structure for the performance. Photograph courtesy of AAS.

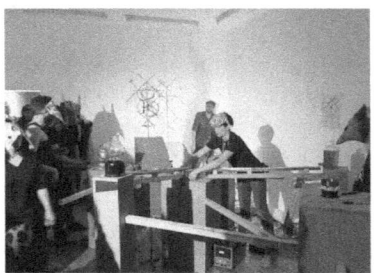

Figure 2.2 Early in the performance of *The Cult of Possible Elements* at
IMT Gallery. Photograph courtesy of AAS and IMT Gallery.

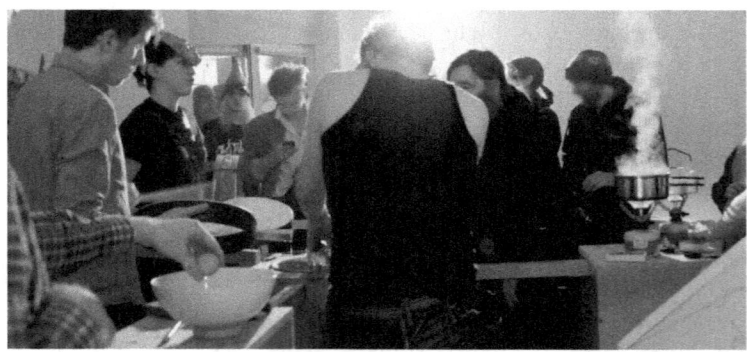

Figure 2.3 Late in the performance of *The Cult of Possible Elements* at
IMT Gallery. Composite still from video courtesy of AAS and
IMT Gallery.

Benlloch: Everyone had their own interests that they were bringing to the project [which] get interconnected and developed into the final score, or plan for what we're doing.

We talk about collaboration as an erasure of sources and authorship. The group generates material that then loses its provenance. Not only does this make concepts free to become attached somewhere new but it binds the group together into a merged community. For Dunning this has mechanical qualities:

Dunning: all of the research gets mangled up and mashed together to the point where nobody can really remember where anything came from but it all seems relevant. [...] In some ways it feels like a musical score where you can improvise and switch instruments, and in some ways like a generative algorithm. [Like] playing improvised music, there's a group and they perform; there's an audience and they watch it but sometimes 'the thing' happens and sometimes it doesn't. [But it can depend] on the audience as well and they become part of the machine by being in the space and watching it.

This kind of practice requires a degree of conviviality. It is not just that there is cooperation amongst the performers, for the performance's success is bound to the presence of an audience. The anticipation of the kinds of audience that might attend a performance is therefore a factor.

Tait: Knowing what kind of audience you're likely to get at IMT you knew that we'd probably be okay to start handing things to the audience members, and so that they become part of the work, whereas other spaces you probably wouldn't want to do that. [And so] people were coming in and we were walking out of the performance persona to just have a chat. This is completely the opposite of performance in that sense. Why shouldn't performance be more egalitarian, more conversational?

Later I will describe how the beginning of IMT was about providing an environment that prioritizes the formation of a new community, what Cooke articulates as: 'to bring new publics into being'.[4] AAS were avoiding the power dynamic of audience participation, but also deliberately stepping away from that viewing of art where the artist and audience are articulated as separate entities, that even when the forth wall is broken that it is clear where the wall (and the break) is. Whereas, in many performances, there is usually a feigning of the lack of knowledge of the audience being there, AAS do this differently here. Here it is more of a community event, rather than art as spectacle. A hybrid of performing/non-performing which, co-opting O'Sullivan's formulation of Laruelle, is an experimentation with the insights and approaches of the former without its inherent hierarchical regulation.

This approach requires a significant amount of trust between artist and gallery:

Dunning:	The key point was that we feel we were trusted. That it was a trusting relationship.
Tait:	I felt [IMT] trusted us to let us get on. You trusting us to not interfere really in what we were doing and trusting us that it's going to be okay. Giving us the space to do it.
Benlloch:	... and trusting the audience as well, that if they did contribute that it would be something that was valuable.

Care is talked a great deal about in terms of curatorial activity, not least due to it being the etymology of curator. But trust is something different, and follows the horizontalism that AAS are prioritizing here:

Benlloch:	It is a more equal relationship, to trust and be trusted. Care implies that [the curator] is a caregiver, and it's a kind of parental role.
Dunning:	... and if we contrast [this performance at IMT] with other places where it hasn't gone as well, that's a big factor. If you feel like they don't trust you to deliver something interesting or something worth

watching, you can end up where it feels combative with the people in authority organising it.

For Tait this trust enables access to the taking of risks, which, he views as a critical component of the performance being part of the world:

Tait: [Trust allows us to] move from a staging of something that already exists, that was rehearsed. [Instead] you *prepare* something, rather than rehearse something, and you allow room within it for things to go wrong. And that's when the thing that's happening now is a *real* thing. And then once one part of the performance is real, it ripples out and everything then becomes real. And if you don't have that trust from the gallery owner or curator, you are not going to be in a position to be able to take that risk.

This trust comes partly through familiarity and mutual interest. We as a gallery and AAS as a collective were seeking similar aims.:

Benlloch: ... we trusted your curatorial vision; the kind of things you'd done in the past.

Tait: It linked to shows before and felt like a thread that runs out into other shows.

Benlloch: ... that kind of finding connections in things, creating meaning out of some kind of similarity, that is a big part of our practice. Taking chance things and acting as if they are significant and building these connections.

Breakdown: There was a diagram that was incomplete and that's what had been done so far, and I remember you'd put some stuff in the diagram and that's the thing that I thought was really good: that the curatorial input was this thing that was comparable to the way the rest of the group was putting stuff in. It was being put in a similar kind of register, which is to say that the information was not really beholden to any overall system.

Benlloch: That performance and the way AAS was working at the time is fairly queer, [and] quite a lot of us had some kind of neurodivergence going on as well – so there is this difference and looking at things in a different way and looking at things from unexpected angles, it's awkward and doesn't fit into the usual categories, it's part of the reflection of the people within it. [It] develops [from how we think].

Tait: ... *divergence*, in a general sense.

Breakdown: All this stuff helps fit the idea of the unique thing of the delivery, and the delivery being the thing that's *taking it seriously*. I think performance is a serious business as it does things to your body as an audience or a participant. There's like the affective register of this stuff that is not easily calculable or is not calculable, and so having a thing where you take that seriously. [...] Improvising is a big part of the AAS structure: you rehearse elements, but you don't rehearse the whole thing. Some of that is going to be dictated by dimensions of the space but also 'how do we feel today? Do we feel like a group that wants to fill the space or do we feel like a group that doesn't?' And we won't know that until we're there. [...] And I really like that as a foundational way of approaching art: taking it seriously but also going 'we can't synthesise this outside of the actual moment'. [...] What is exciting about art is that it's not a thing that can be nailed down as a fixed definition, but you have to find ways of working with it while it is still alive and slippery. [...] Through mutual support and dialogue, you can develop this: 'We're going to help you see what art you can make under these conditions'.

Breakdown is also talking about making art as something that happens *now*. Exhibitions, unlike artworks, were not made to last. They were made to be temporary. These are not 'current trends', but actual currents (flows) moving as the work is being experienced. Here there is a holding pattern in which the normal hierarchies and thresholds of gallery, curator, artist, visitor are unsettled. An opening up of a closed entity of the work into a diagram that is maintained instead through its relations, its freedom to drift from the tradition of a contained entity into an environment of past and future projects, between hosts, artists, and audience. This interest for AAS is visible in part through their interest in improvisation. They deploy improvisatory traditions coming from the concerns of rhizomatic music, and these traditions are political, as Gilbert clarifies of Attali, in their refusal of the mechanisms produced by 'individualisation of power and expression' and the 'stratified hierarchies of the orchestra [as] a metaphor for a hierarchically stratified society' (Attali in Gilbert 2004:127). This refusal amounts to a desire to imagine a more horizontal relationship between organizers, creators, and audiences of an event, and allows the curatorial, the gallery itself, to fold into the work.

The dissolution of the curator in *Cult of Possible Elements* can be read as a readjustment of traditional hierarchies that were previously locked into place. Professionally curators are trusted to be confident in their expertise, whereas in a project like *The Cult of Possible Elements*, one must be confident in one's lack of expertise, being aware of what the artists are about but at the same time committing oneself with a degree of ignorance and a lack of power or control over an idea. Being in a position as a curator where I feel unprepared, inexpert, and yet involved.

It is through projects such as *The Cult of Possible Elements* that we are able to explore less stratified configurations of consumption and production and allow some expansion of consumption/production configurations of artists. Here the gallery undoes its self-proclaimed role of organization subtracting territories from artists' activity, and more a resource to, in Breakdown's formulation, 'help you see what art you can make under these conditions'. Here, perhaps, the effect is that the limits of roles are negated, the aim of which being to generate the possibility of new relations, and new affects, that would otherwise be marginalized or refused.

Notes

1 For this event Plastique Fantastique were David Burrows, Alex Marzeta, Simon O'Sullivan, and Vanessa Page.
2 The inaugural fair of a London art fair that ran from 2013 to 2016 before going on extended hiatus.
3 This summary and the conversation that follows are from two 2021 conversations over Zoom around the 2013 event, the first with Ana Benlloch, Graham Dunning and Stuart Tait (14 October), and the second with Uma Breakdown (25 October).
4 2022 IMT Zoom meeting, 9 August.

3   This Is a Not-Me

Prior to March 2020, IMT had had a good year. We had, in 2019, been selected for Art Rotterdam and sold well.[1] This then followed with a series of well-received exhibitions *Snow Crash*, curated by Cooke, *Plastique Fantastique: Zer0 City* and *Benedict Drew: Trapped in a Sticky Shed with Side Chain Compression*,[2] and in 2020 had launched *Givin u coy givin u smize*.[3] Friend was working on sales from previous exhibitions and had organized visits with potential collectors. Then the first of the UK COVID-19 lockdowns was announced, and it became clear that we would need to entirely re-evaluate what it was that IMT would be doing during the pandemic. There was the key question of whether we needed a show during the pandemic, whether art could still be useful to people at that time. It was clear that the work of the gallery was geared towards the assumed value of audiences experiencing art, and in recognizing the totalizing imposition of digital technology in the mediation of our making. What would the kind of gallery described above do in the context of lockdown? The Arts Council England had announced a fund, the Emergency Response Fund for non-NPOs[4] and so, if IMT could survive as an entity regardless of whether it was to receive this funding, we should channel some of that support to artists who were all in precarious situations.[5]

I was approached by LUVA Gallery for an interview about *This Is a Not-Me* for their June 2021 zine. I reproduce parts of that interview here:

DOI: 10.4324/9781003197959-4

Lindsay and I had already committed to help IMT keep going through the pandemic with our own resources from other jobs, so we wanted to get as much of [the Emergency Response Fund] to artists as seemed feasible in the form of commissions. But, we also wanted to make sure that we had some kind of existence, outside of being basically a temporary storage facility for the duration of lockdown. Early on, I was thinking about artists who couldn't access their studios, who'd had projects cancelled and who were worried about income, so the project started from that point. Artists were suddenly deprived of materials and practices that were important to their working processes. For artists like Plastique Fantastique (for whom being in the same space, doing things together, is such an important part of what they do), it was a recognition that this was not business as usual. There were also artists that we'd started working with on other things that had to be put on hold.

(Rohtmaa-Jackson in Poole 2021:2)

We were in a relatively good position for a pandemic exhibition, we had had a series of exhibition themed around viruses, apocalypse, SHTF/TEOTWAWKI[6] survivalism, and post-humanism.[7] We also, as a gallery, had technical experience. Many artists we'd worked with used digital media in part or all of their practice and as a gallery we'd begun using social media relatively early, adopting a MySpace account and, in 2008, a Flickr,[8] before moving on to Twitter, Instagram, Facebook, YouTube, and others. I had also, as an artist, been a contributor to a series of streaming exhibitions for Emily Webber and Amy Cunningham' s online arts environment *not-TV* (2000–2), which may have, subconsciously, contributed to *This Is a Not-Me*'s title.

The title is often the first port of call for an exhibition and presents the contextualization of the show with the terms of the title and any potential rationale for these terms. Both in *not-TV* and *This Is a Not-Me*, a refusal to declare what the subject as a title is, but rather what this subject isn't, is immediately disruptive of this process. But the title also comes through the division between our physical selves and their images on social media, how there are images of us out there, complete with algorithmical desires, that are *of* us but *not* us.

The public spaces that became most visible in the UK during the isolation of the pandemic lockdowns were, of course, spaces offered and controlled by US businesses: social media networks supported mainly by advertising revenue. The title related to the anxieties of isolation as well as the anxieties of social media as a potentially maladaptive solution, especially when social media profiles suddenly must carry all that extra baggage of our isolation. And:

> when software like Facebook stakes a claim over words that actually matter to who we are as organic beings, like 'memories' and 'friends', and turns them into cloud storage. So the exhibition title was a reflection of these things.
>
> (ibid.)

The project was to reflect anxieties of being visible as a digital entity whilst having no access to other spaces, being mindful that social media's reflection of our various life states may obscure some of the more affective presences that impact on our lives. In the social digital, the threshold between work and life is gone and the images we must present are smiles (Fisher 2018:535–7):

> Online activity has entirely different relationships to speed; subjectivity; attention; the honesty of interactions; the pause between thinking and commenting; and work/life balance. [...] Social media instinctively consumes our non-work lives and grinds it together with obligation, self-surveillance and professional anxiety.
>
> (Rohtmaa-Jackson in Poole 2021:5)

Additionally, for IMT, the pandemic arrived at a time when art has come from a position of saying it is a social solution, a means of unravelling patriarchy, Western-centred modes, and therapeutics. But its presence on social media instead foregrounds FOMO anxiety, the proliferation of representation over work viewed in its material conditions, a narrative more of lack than desire. In their essay on the implications of social media, McKinnon returns to the myth of Narcissus, noting how '*narcissism* has the same root as *narcosis*, from *narke*, or "numbness". Could it be that we have misunderstood the myth of Narcissus? Perhaps it is not *self-love*, but [...] *self-loss* [...] an emptying out of affect' (2022). If McKinnon is right, what purpose would such software have? In 1967 a Doctor Who serial, staring Patrick Troughton, aired on BBC television called *The Evil of the Daleks*. Written by David Whitaker it reimagines the quasi-fascist cyborg aliens as manipulators seeking to understand what made humans (which we are expected to assume are non-fascists or less-fascist) so successful in their victories against them. They seek to implant human behaviours (in *The Evil of the Daleks* this is described as the 'human factor') into test daleks. What this story does is not make machines to help humans (the main assumption of technology, from pre-history to cyberpunk) but instead seeks to make humans help machines. Through online work meetings during a pandemic, more of us gave up our identities, our homes, health vulnerabilities, and private responsibilities of care to this machine. 'Our work, and the economy, has after all been declared more important than our survival' (Rohtmaa-Jackson in Poole 2021:11).

One of the principal criticisms of online gallery activity during the COVID lockdown was the idea of a cultural glut of information, what Walsh calls, 'the immeasurable quantity of artistic activity and its dissemination on [social media] platforms' (Walsh 2021:8). Some commentators (Walsh [2021] and Quaintance [2020b], for example) describe how the anxiety of this glut and the language of attention is problematic in the simplicity of its circulation. On the one hand, this shock is really a shock that there are galleries that have always been everywhere regularly making exhibitions, that there are too many to see, and that the business of galleries making projects is easier to filter out when you can't easily visit them. Whereas the ease of access to online material and, often, the replicability of some projects weighs heavily on an online audience with a stake in art world visibility. There is, especially in Walsh's review, an amplification of Groys' identification that the content is outgrowing the audience: that there are more content creators than viewers (Groys 2009).

There was also the clear, to me, absurdity of galleries appearing to suggest that their online spaces were replications of their bricks and mortar spaces. Instagram, Twitch, YouTube, et al. are not gallery spaces, but companies with their own contracts, ethics, and control, even more geared to the moderating influence of capital

(Ziherl 2016). We are having to play by the rules of the platforms, and what content (especially what bodies and politics) that, from their reading of it, can be deemed appropriate for public attention.

This invasion of privacy in a mediascape of lack, the media saturation of a web-centric social and professional life, and the yielding of editorial control to international software companies were the starting conditions of *This Is a Not-Me*. It was clear that any project would need to be flexible to cater for artists' life circumstances as well as critical of the very platforms it was using to disseminate their work. Collaborative projects like *Cult of Possible Elements* had begun the work of destabilizing the curator-as-auteur, *This Is a Not-Me* was to foreground the collaborative as a meant to continuously destabilize the expectations of its field.

This is a Not-Me was an exhibition with Kara Chin, Gentle Stranger, Felix Rose Kawitzky, Plastique Fantastique, John Powell-Jones, Frankie Roberts, Maggie Roberts, and Thomson and Craighead. As a work about simulation, Disney seemed an appropriate context both as Baudrillard's reference for simulation as a producer of virtuality (Baudrillard 1996), but also as streaming services, such as Disney+, were a new focus for entertainment during pandemic lockdowns. For *This Is A Not-Me*'s key text I proposed Disney's *High School Musical 2* (2007), which articulated a particular articulation of time, work, and friendship that encapsulated both social media and UK government narrative that stressed work and maintaining the economy as the key aim. In *High School Musical 2*, the characters sing, 'We've got to work, work, to work this out, we'll make things right, the sun will shine', a refrain that I felt resonated with *The Wicker Man* (1973) in which human sacrifice is deemed necessary for a good harvest.

Having provided a key text, the project then was to develop through group Zoom meetings with the artists. Conscious of pandemic-effected time commitments and other individual circumstances, I felt that the curatorial methodology should centre ongoing group conversations. The artists all brought key reference points to these conversations which would then impact on the work of others.

This Is a Not-Me's curatorial design was going to respond to its ethical position. It was going to start as a series of group meetings via Zoom, be an inter-generational approach to exhibition building, allowing emerging and more established artists to support each other, and was going to respond to the improvisatory nature of the kinds of collaboration we'd become familiar with through a curatorial strategy we'd developed through working with Plastique Fantastique and ASS. As such, *This Is a Not-Me* started as this exhibition that was going to be sporadic in both the timing of its public outputs and the platforms they would appear on, decentralized via Instagram, Twitch, Discord, WhatsApp as well as IMT's and the artists' own websites and social media accounts. It was to be led more by each artists' ability to be part of it over the next six months rather than curatorial or institutional demand:

> Maggie Roberts: *This is a Not-Me* [...] as a response to COVID and isolation [...] created a sort of intimacy in screen. [IMT] made zoom a space that we all came together organically, we'd never normally have that opportunity. Normally you're in a group show, you deliver the work, perhaps you get involved in the installation, that's it. One of the things for me that's precious about that show is the word intimacy [...] you made this space where we kind of got to play together. Lindsay [Friend] became a complete genius on how to use social media in ways that was giving it a power that wasn't marketing. We had a real dialogue between the media that we're usually so disparaging about. It was an energetic a live space.
>
> (Roberts 2021, personal communication, 13 January)

The project explored how social media mediates our understanding of the world and asked questions around what its immediacy is about. It tried to determine how we can use it to create community, under the conditions of its unceasing surveillance, rather than define human use in the economy. Social media in its enormity offers myriad differing perspectives and critiques at terrifying speed, and it is easy to channel this criticism directly into our lives: how we look, what we wear, what we think, what we have done and intend to do. This is a challenge first and foremost of visibility.

This challenge of excess visibility can impact on experimental activity (trying things out without knowing where they might end up). Anxieties over the critical responses of those we follow (whether friends, professional acquaintances, or idols) and of those who are brought into our feed *by* those we follow, in a visible environment that sees and comments on process as it happens, can impact on the work. Sometimes this interrogation is useful, sometimes it is necessary, but sometimes it can create a kind of paralysis or conformity.

As the COVID-19 lockdown forced individuals to increase screentime and socially engage via distance, this seemed like a potential threat to experimental art-making. We can see this in art studios at universities as students become paralysed from making in fear of the polyphony of social media that runs a relentless, charismatic, and personalized feed on how the world should be remade, a feed that is often contradictory, rhetorical and necessarily oversimplified and linked to high stakes (i.e. routine personal decisions linked to apocalyptic climate collapse). As an attempt to provide a solution, *This Is a Not-Me* turned these tools into supporting a community of artists to build a show. Maggie Roberts' *Meditations* series and Felix Rose Kawitzky's *Otherwards* were exemplars of this, both creating communities in themselves in which audience, artist, and performer were in flux around an art object that was unclear in itself: *Otherwards* being a queer world-building exercise using Discord to bring viewers into a making, and *Octopus Meditations* using group meditation exercise as form.

Crucially this horizontalism seems to be a potential function of the technologies adopted as part of the COVID response, digital space offering opportunity for artist-led projects.

These things, horizontalism, collaboration, trust and intimacy, experimentalism, and improvisation although especially visible in the above two projects regularly come out of IMT's curatorial activity regardless of who, individually, is curating the exhibitions. From this I shall examine how IMT gave rise to these conditions. *This Is a Not-Me* created a hybrid of many:

> A new kind of creature, built on Zoom. We are part bird, part human, part many other things […] we start to declare our individual updates over the top of one another as each appears in the story, different worlds, different timelines existing side-by-side.
>
> (Rohtmaa-Jackson 2020)

What is IMT as a new kind of creature?

Notes

1 Featuring a solo presentation of work by Paola Ciarska.
2 The essay IMT had commissioned from Kristen Gallerneaux for *Trapped in a Sticky Shed with Side Chain Compression* can be found in Sutcliffe (2021).
3 Paola Ciarska, Sadé Mica, and Salut C'est Cool.
4 Arts organizations that were not part of their National Portfolio of annually funded organizations.
5 Since then it has become clear that others felt the same. Anne Duffau, Hana Noorali, and Tai Shani would subsequently launch Transmissions in part to find a way to create an opportunity to direct financial support from arts budgets straight to artists, curators, or thinkers.
6 Shit hits the fan/the end of the world as we know it.
7 Including Suzanne Treister's *Works from SURVIVOR (F)* (2017), Linda Stupart with Ray Filar's *After the Ice, the Deluge* (2017) and *Feeling Safer* (2016).
8 Some remanences of which still survives at www.flickr.com/people/imt gallery/

4   Five Mouths that Form a Diagram of Desire

For Serres there are two mouths. The first of language and accumulation, and a second that tastes, hidden under 'the weight of logic and grammar' (Serres 1985:235). We instead anticipate five mouths. Five with candy moving between them. For we want to think about curating a different way.[1]

The first mouth: *Joshua Cohen tells a story about a sliver of Einstein's brain in a jar of formaldehyde in the possession of William Burroughs. It passes to a new owner and becomes a charm: 'you scooped the bit of Einstein's brain out of the jar and shook off the excess formaldehyde; then [...] sucked on the brain-bit until your mouth went numb – until the formaldehyde paralyzed your lips and tongue and you couldn't be understood, you couldn't even feel yourself trying to make language' (Cohen 2020). This mouth is the chrysostomos; the loud mouth; the mouth of language. It is the mouth of accumulation and of money.*

The second mouth: *It is 2020 and also 1991. In Carmen Maria Machado's* In the Dream House *(2020) Machado visits the Brooklyn Museum to see* HIDE/SEEK: Difference and Desire in American Portraiture. *They take a candy from the pile that is Félix González-Torres'* Untitled (Portrait of Ross in LA) *(1991). They describe its coded meaning as a disappearing body, framed by the writer trapped in a vicious, abusive relationship (Machado 2020:137–8). They describe the relation of human beings to art, how we carry our relationships past and present with us even then. This mouth is thought entangled with sensation; sensation with thought.*

DOI: 10.4324/9781003197959-5

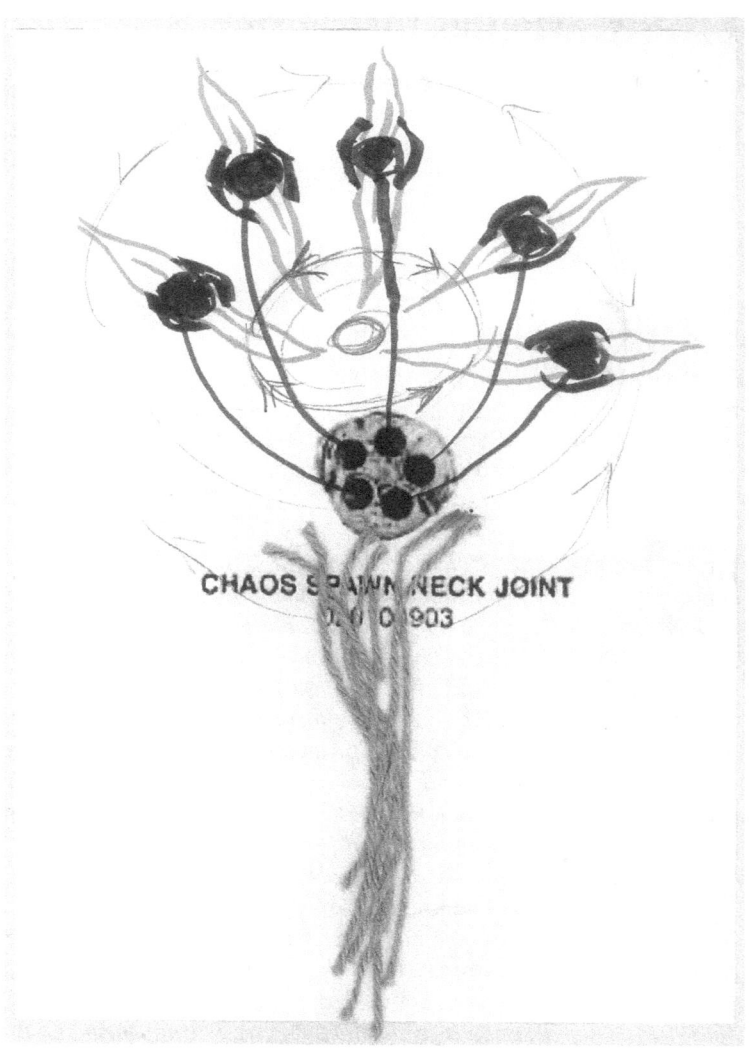

Figure 4.1 A diagram of five mouths.

The third mouth: *It is 1993 and also before this. Whitley Streiber reads books in his library. In his mouth is a half-sucked candy. He reads the* Tao Te Ching *and the Gospels, and* Life Between Life *by Dr Joel Whitton and Joe Fisher, a book about bardo, a liminal state in some schools of Buddhism said to exist between death and rebirth. These books have been suggested by a Visitor from another world. The candy Streiber is sucking is one the Visitor left behind; half finished, moulded by the architecture of their mouth, soaked in their saliva. Streiber will write about this experience in a chapter titled 'In the Nature of Joy' (Streiber 1995:197–207). This mouth is the desire to know and love a stranger.*

The fourth mouth: *It is 1985. In* Friday 13th Part V: A New Beginning *a boy in care eats candy, chocolate all around his mouth. The boy is a cipher, lazily coded as overweight, greedy, guileless, and lacking in critical thinking. A convenient victim to lend cause to the film's twist that the killer is not who we think. The boy is dead before the candy reaches his stomach. He tastes it but it doesn't nourish him. This mouth is a hunger for something we can never have. A zombie formulation: hungry but never full.*

The fifth mouth: *It is 1989 and it is also the turn of the 42nd millennium. Alien creatures called Genestealers arrive in vast hulks of cut-up derelict spacecraft. Their sharp tongues implant eggs under the skin of fascists to create human–alien hybrids. The egg is a jumble of possibilities. The fascist is law and structure and death. This mouth is the egg discourse for the proliferation of hybrids.*

These five mouths form the upper limits of a hybrid creature, part Penanggalan, part Lernaean Hydra, part Kraat. It is a spirit summoned to do work for us. It protects, harms enemies, and has the power to regenerate its wounds. Stats for this creature will be made available in a forthcoming supplement.

Note

1 Despite apparent semantic corelation, I think these five mouths are only serendipitously connected to Simon O'Sullivan's essay 'Fictioning Five Heads: (on the Art—Anthropology Hybrid)' (2018) in Hermione Spriggs, H. (ed.) *Five Heads (Tavan Tolgoi): Art, Anthropology and Mongol Futurism*, Berlin: Steernberg; Five Heads, who miraculously,

and marvellously, materialized on my reading list after the Penanggalan had spontaneously manifested. At least, I *think* it was that was round. Who knows. I may have seen Simon tweet or otherwise share this essay whilst I doom-scrolled, and maybe that was why these mouths seemed so right.

5 Hybrid Eggs and Deterritorialization

Towers Open Fire (1963) is a film by Antony Balch, based on Burroughs' cut-up trilogy in which hipsters occupy and repurpose the technologies of media visibility. These hipsters use this repurposing to disrupt control, causality, and a pre-written news agenda.

Tower Open Fire is a dream text for IMT, but other spaces have deployed similar objectives. Gavin Wade of Eastside Projects in Birmingham posits a similar aim in the 'Eastside Projects Requirements' sent to the artists Joanne Tatham and Tom O'Sullivan in 2009 and published in their book *Amongst Other Things an Unsuccessful Proposal for the 2012 Cultural Olympiad* (2013). Wade asks that together the artists and Eastside Projects 'execute functional constructions and alter or refurbish existing structures as a means of surviving in a capitalist economy [...] to keep at bay the monopoly of cultural homogeneity' and maintain that the gallery is 'not a standard but a model to be adapted and exploited' (9–10). Like the hipsters of *Towers Open Fire*, Eastside is aware of an enemy that is a corporate system intent on a uniformity. They see survival as the challenge and structures as resources to be utilized to this end, and, importantly, that their own operation becomes a model for subsequent exploitation by others also to this end. Here artist-run spaces see gallery infrastructure as an opportunity to remix into something more in-line with political objectives than financial ones, but equally, by having an eye on sustainability, this has created a powerful ecosystem of alternative institutions.

DOI: 10.4324/9781003197959-6

The climactic twist of *Towers Open Fire*: a triumphant, dancing hipster is surprised by the invention of colour film, a new technology of control. As art school graduates we were nurtured in postmodernism, told by our universities that education brings power and by our lecturers, via Foucault or Said, that power is maintained and protected by the persistence of grand narratives. In *Towers Open Fire*, technologies become cheap enough to access and grant agency, until they are improved, become out of reach, and our lack of access becomes an indicator of our lack of power. This is a reading from a capitalist art world. Later, in this text, Robakowski's *Kiner* will tell a similar story from a communist one.

Let's assume IMT's aims are about deterritorialzing (as per: Deleuze and Guattari). A glance at some exhibition press releases (the primary public emergence of a new exhibition) reveals a use of language that is intentionally subverting of expectations (whether twisting art speak or using slang). This is and was intentionally destabilizing, intentionally seeking to create friction from within settled organizational structures. The information text for the exhibition *Alternative 23* (IMT 2014, Gallery North 2015, and Worcester City Gallery/Perrins Gallery, Worcester 2015) uses this approach to describe multiplicities, needlessly revelling in and aestheticizing violence and gore in the spirit of comics like *2000 AD* and body horror movies:

> slasher-physics and slasher-politics […] killed, cut into pieces, minced and yet new; beheading, disembowelling, freezing and shattering, skewering through genitals, snapping in half and concussing into mulch […] pulp forms [of] an old world mapped onto the new one.
>
> (Jackson 2014a)

Or in *Polymorph Other* where the visitor, the reader of the text, is expected to be implicated in how the exhibition plays out:

> One Thursday evening at IMT Gallery, YOU will track down the villain! Travel the great spaceways of the Blue Mountain, enter the deep caverns of the Dice Cult, explore the sociopolitical undercurrents of an experimental World War II psychiatric rehabilitation camp! Your mission: to search for an answer to the ever-growing threat of the Present Continuum!
>
> (Hughes and Jackson 2018)

However, the deterritorializing of gallery limits and functions, especially their stability, may be a strategic goal in theory, and it is part of becoming-gallery (and a deterritorializing of subjectivity that would entail), but *in practice* this is messier. In fact, the gallery was both a scramble for structure and a scrambling *of* structures. As Sansone Ruiz summarized in terms of her impression of IMT,

> [You] think expansively and widely and deeply about certain histories of art practices. There's a lot of education, a lot of sensitivity and thought and consideration. It's actually an incredibly well-oiled machine that's just ... really okay with experimentation. Lindsay hits her marks. She gets the applications in. The work is framed properly. She's done her research. It only really works because the person actually knows the rules and can hit her marks very well. And then has the space to make a fucking mess of it.
>
> (Sansone Ruiz 2021, personal communication, 12 October)

The mess is internecine. The mess is, as Nicole's point intended it to be, the actual success of IMT in the mode Deleuze defines in terms of the schizophrenic in his distinction between paranoia and schizophrenia, paranoia as the production of territories through restoring codes, and schizophrenia as producing lines of flight, a taking apart and assembling and deterritorialization. IMT is relational, not essential. Not fixed. So then what is IMT trying to do? If it is really a hybrid, it is with the aim of being in a state in which it remains unable to be co-opted by a particular system or structure and remaining unsettled.

So a hybrid space is a project in that we are applying project-based rules to the exploration of a field with the sense that there is a temporariness to it for as O'Doherty maintains, a project ends (1999:70). A knowing that the project will succeed or fail and at either point becomes something else. This temporariness is being unsettled. It must be temporary, or it wouldn't be hybrid. In this sense it is like the collective, denoted by the quasi-object of Serres, which 'when being passed, makes the collective, if it stops, it makes the individual. If he is discovered, he is "it" [also translatable as 'dead']' (Serres 1982:225).

But this is not the only form of hybridity that IMT takes. This is in part the hybrid of business models: the non-profit, garage, artist-run amalgam of desires, and the commercial/art-market model, but this simple dualism doesn't encapsulate the proliferating hybridity of the *Space Hulk* hybrid, of the fifth mouth. But nested within that is another hybrid: a hybrid of subjectivities. The idea space of the hybrid of the fifth mouth is a diagrammatic flow of alien to hybrid, an access to and control of the technologies and actions of the hybrid by the alien. This idea space is what Burroughs and Bryon Gysin called 'the Third Mind' (1978), a hybrid as a creative force, made from two-plus subjectivities. It is where these two diagrams overlap that I ultimately understand the flows and manifestations of the gallery as a hybrid taking place.

6   Gallery as Third Mind

Napolean Hill's self-help book *Think and Grow Rich*, first published during the Great Depression, offers the idea of a 'Master Mind' as the ninth of its 'Thirteen Steps to Riches' as: the 'Coordination of knowledge and effort, in a spirit of harmony, between two or more people, for the attainment of a definite purpose' (Hill 1937:178). This collaborative intelligence is, claims Hill, the only route to accumulating 'GREAT POWER' (ibid. 179). Hill's Master Mind became a model for Burroughs and Gysin to develop through esoteric reworkings of the metaphysics of Dianetics and Scientology (Jackson 2014b) into their concept of what they'd call the Third Mind. Burroughs describes the Third Mind as: 'the complete fusion in a praxis of two subjectivities, two subjectivities that metamorphose into a third; it is from this collusion that a new author emerges, an absent third person, invisible and beyond grasp, decoding the silence' (Burroughs and Gysin 1978:18). For Burroughs, the Third Mind is a going 'outward' (ibid.:2) without words, without the first mouth of hegemonic *talk*, in the manner of a diagram: a structure through which concepts might be interacted with or decoded by collaboration, and through which new trajectories might be negotiated. The Third Mind is a mind of its own, separate from the minds that manifest it.

The first public positioning of IMT as explicitly a Third Mind came at a talk I gave at the Conference for Emerging Art Organisers, Goldsmiths, in 2011: '[IMT was] founded to be, in essence, a collaborative process', and that we understood this collaboration via the Third Mind, as an entity that could access places the individuals contributing to it couldn't reach individually, in how it

DOI: 10.4324/9781003197959-7

decodes the silence in artistic collaborations and cultural production. So, for me, IMT Gallery is a Third [Mind, and *as* a
Third Mind], the gallery provides a domain in which [the] needs
and interactions [of artists and partner organizations] can be
played out.

Because IMT is a Third Mind, IMT is also a type of social practice
in the Chris Kraus sense, as a 'confluence of mutual self interest'
(Kraus 2018:29). Friend and others, coming together as a *scene*.

In synergy with Burroughs and Gysin's deploying of the Third
Mind, these are the processes by which this silence, this space of
potentialities, is reached. These involve evident methodological
curatorial forms drawn directly from Burroughs' writing and cyber-
netic, magickal practice: cut-up, fold-in, smudging (manipulating
sounds on audiotape recordings) and, by extension, breaking into
the Reality Studio to mess with the tapes. These techniques are
alchemical: Burroughs' theorizing follows the line that by manipulating representations (words, symbols, recordings, images) you
manipulate the thing represented, the material object or event.
These processes are explicitly about using the technology and
infrastructures of 'the Boards, Syndicates and Governments of the
Earth' against those systems, rewriting them in often chaotic and
arbitrary ways, and it is from this that we conceptualized IMT's
hybridity as well as its curatorial methodology: a metamodelized
production of new assemblages from existing models and/or the
internecine making of 'a fucking mess of it'.

In 'Silver Smoke of Dreams', a tape experiment from the
early 1960s released on *Break Through in Grey Room* (1986b),
Burroughs and Ian Summerville repeat the phrase 'hello, yes,
hello' as an exercise 'simply to record the basic communication formula and then smudge it'. 'Hello yes hello' is a phrase
Burroughs takes from a Dianetics/Scientology exercise which he
describes in a letter (13 December 1965) to Antony Balch as 'I
communicate acknowledge communication and communicate
back' (Morgan 2012:205).[1] Smudging throws our truth positions
as curators into doubt, into smudges and fragments. It writes
IMT's programme and individual kooky exhibition ideas as a
way of constructing a secret history and give alternate readings
of contemporary trends and synergies, smudging the utterances
of the first mouth.

As our trajectory came more via Burroughs than via psychoanalysis and schizoanalysis, IMT was consciously less about making holes and more about cutting up and smudging.² That said, the folding together of the Freudian psychotic subject as a body full of holes, and the Deleuze schizophrenic subject as a production of rationalizations, goes some way to articulate how Lindsay and I understood IMT as a Third Mind, albeit one that produces implications not entitlements and whose vulnerability we might register if only as an artificial subjectivity.

IMT as Third Mind, as an architectural space conflating, as Burroughs does, the inner and outer (Burroughs 1985:16), as well as the gallery's work/home hybridity (which I outline in Chapter 12) begs, at least to me, esoteric confluence with Oldenburg's 'Third Place' (1989), but the Third Place is neither work nor home, whereas IMT is both of these. Perhaps the heterotopia of Soja's 'Thirdspace' in which

> everything comes together … subjectivity and objectivity, the abstract and the concrete, the real and the imagined, the knowable and the unimaginable, the repetitive and the differential, structure and agency, mind and body, consciousness and the unconscious, the disciplined and the transdisciplinary, everyday life and unending history.
>
> (1996:57)

The five-mouth model is not based on anything sustainable; it is always up in the air. The Penangallen is in a constant state of hyperarousal, caught between home, work, and the third. And the demand of the five mouths is, like the zombie's hunger, a desire that never equates to a balancing sustenance. Again, internecine. Our mental health and the kinds of working practices that fit around this kind of hybridity might at any point hasten a fatal collapse, moving at the wrong speed, leading to disintegration or institutionalization (see Deleuze 2003). There is a risk, with this merging, that a body in the live/work hybrid loses its identity to the gallery, that nerves become digital networks and blood becomes matt white emulsion. The gallery is as fragile as human bodies.

The difference in origin of schizoanalysis (an attempt to understand desire in the context of capitalism) and the origin of the Third Mind (a popular self-help guide to business) is perhaps revealing of why we found ourselves manifesting the latter. Yet the Third Mind, as we understood it, is resolutely a diagram in that it is a structure formed through relations and flows, and we would deploy it in those terms. Like Burrows and O'Sullivan's interest with Plastique Fantastique, we are also attempting a practice whose criticality is based on a cutting up or production of holes (Burrows and O'Sullivan 2014:266), a relationship to the systems on which we, as an organization, rely.[3]

Working with IMT at the start of 2019, curating *Snow Crash*, and then later joining as co-curator in 2020, Cooke brings a compelling framing of this curatorial mode of repurposing technologies. For Cooke, this comes from their reading of Keller Easterling's *Extrastatecraft* (2016) and how Easterling describes infrastructure space and talks about 'disposition' in terms of how corporations fiction themselves.

For Cooke, Easterling's observations contribute to the principle that the world is being fictioned by those that have the power to do so. And 'if the world is being fictioned, because we know that mediation is everywhere and we are fictioning our interaction with the world, how do we fiction it differently?' (Cooke 2021, personal communication, 2 December). Cooke's concern is to make sure we stage disposition within the exhibitions we build:

> Staging the disposition alongside the mediation so that we can see this tension between us, the tension of making something that is complex and retains the distinctness between its actors, whilst also bringing them together. Because they are conveying really important information and thoughts and feelings about being a body in the contemporary infrastructures, and maybe a body that isn't meant for those structures.
>
> (ibid.)

For Cooke the concern is urgent for the infrastructures we move within are not built for the different bodies that make up the world, but are built for white, male, middle-class, Western bodies. As Cooke explains, even if this standard is not representative of who we are:

> what happens to the people that are in the central matrix of power that want to resist those structures? I think that how

those who are in the central matrix of power resist them is by using the very tools against themselves.

(ibid.)

For Cooke they are in agreement with Walter Mignolo in a need to sustain different logic systems, however whilst Mignolo argues that this must be done in borders, researching and rethinking histories that might provide this, Cooke is concerned with how one also does this from the position of relative power without a history or cultural alternative to the capitalism we might have been brought up in. Cooke's answer is 'the only thing we can do is rewire it and give a space for different voices and technological systems to emerge'. (ibid.)

This strategy is part of a network of resistance and retaliation. This co-opting has synergies to anarchism, according to Lauder:

The state is not something which can be destroyed by a revolution, but is a condition, a certain relationship between human beings, a mode of human behaviour; we destroy it by contracting other relationships, by behaving differently.

(Landauer in Ward 2004:8)

As well as feminist organizing (Hester 2018 and Jury et al. 2018), and a queer rejection of the binary:

When we reject the binary, we reject the economy that goes along with it. When we reject the binary, we challenge how we're valued in a capitalist society that yokes our gender to the labor we enact. When we reject the binary we claim uselessness as a strategic tool.

(Russell 2020:69)

And Cooke's take here also has synergies with the cut-up repurposing of Burroughs: seeking a truth of intention (or disposition, for Easterling) through cutting up and rearranging the materials of power, and by doing so finding new juxtapositions that might result in access to space.

However, although I have claimed for IMT a degree of periphery (a periphery from the mythical centre of the art world), it is difficult not to see ourselves from certain perspectives as wielding a degree of established power both through the location of IMT, as described later in this book, and the accumulation of cultural capital. For Cooke, part of the issue is the problem articulated in Gayatri Chakravorty Spivak's 'Can the Subaltern Speak?', or in the work of Franz Fanon: 'If you move into the centre to gain access to power, then you change. You're not the original voice anymore (if there ever is one)'. Cooke's strategy is one of metamodelization: 'What you have to do, is look at the system itself and try and manipulate it so that it becomes flexible to these different bodies and voices' (Cooke 2021, personal communication, 2 December).

However, Cooke's rewiring might also be understood as a form of marginalization that evokes a cultural character that *is* present in the histories and cultures under capitalism: that of the trickster. Ruth Catlow and Penny Rafferty explicitly declare their Decentralised Autonomous Organisations as trickster (Catlow and Rafferty 2022:13) and go on to describe ways in which such a mode can reveal the operations of power whilst also creating alternative visions of the future (ibid. 2022). Ana Benlloch and Stuart Tait of the artist collective AAS view IMT's activities as comparable to the trickster mode of organizing in the context of George Hansen's formulation of the 'trickster organisation' in *The Trickster and the Paranormal* (Hansen 2001). For Hansen, the trickster is 'a constellation of abstract qualities [that do] not subscribe to Western logic [and so] may seem jumpy, jarring and not quite coherent' (ibid. 36) and this can extend to organizations, a kind of 'anti-structural' organization (and how this anti-structure reflects work with the paranormal) that repurposes the structures and languages of mainstream culture (normal as opposed to paranormal) and makes 'bizarre claims that [provoke] ridicule and [bring] discredit upon them' (ibid. 170). For Hansen, this is the appearance of the trickster who induces marginality. The implication here is that IMT (characterized as I have done here in its hybridity) induces its own marginality, and this marginality is in relation to society that it interacts with, as well as in relation to the art world that it is seen as a part of. Although this might be an extreme case for IMT, I'd argue that this is a relation common in many small galleries that exhibit some form of Third Mind hybridity. This might especially be the case with what is referred to as 'artist-run' galleries.

Galleries like IMT that feel unattached from and unsupported by the art world and experience the exploitation by institutions and their own anxious efficiency can give us pause that such venal mimicry isn't ethical. And, as Tai Shani has argued, albeit regarding a far more urgent and intense context, it is the ethical refusal of artists that can be their only agency:

> The only meaningful action artists have in the face of huge networks of power and systemic injustice is the right of refusal. Especially when all the structures that benefit from not only our work, but also our politics, leave us ethically vulnerable.[4]
>
> (Shani 2022)

Given this, it is unsurprising that artist-run projects often articulate their activities as critical of power, and this agency is often mimicked and performed by organizations that seek radicality and relevance (Russell 2022, Raicovich 2021, Quaintance 2020a and 2021, Hylton 2007, and de Mille in ICA 2016). IMT must tread carefully. We seek the exciting possibilities of creative, unsettled hybridity (the gallery as a production–contingency assemblage), yet our relation to the institution must always be one of antagonism. The third is a creature of mouths; never settled.

Notes

1 A similar exercise is conducted between Christopher Walken (as Whitley Strieber) as he tries to communicate with his alien abductors, the Blue Doctors, in the 1989 movie *Communion* (based on Strieber's 1987 memoir *Communion: A True Story*). In the case of the Doctors the exercise is a series of hand gesture greetings performed back and forth between the Doctors and Strieber as they greet and/or begin to process him: first a bow whilst rolling hands over one another; followed by a bow with a hand motion to the side; a bow and palms pressed together (a silent namaste); a bow touching the forehead and then chest, repeated once; a long handshake, at the end of which the Blue Doctor cocks a snook; and lastly a low five, reciprocated. It's a useful system for all gallery invigilators to commit to memory and bring out when needed.

2 That said, the vinyl record I made released comprised of ambient excerpts of an unpublished interview with Burroughs in his final years by the writer Roger Clarke, was exactly that: a series of holes made in the expectations of a voice (Jackson 2014c).

3 A vivid example of utilizing diagrams as a curatorial practice that incorporates some of the same registers yet develops them in a significantly more focused manner can be found in Lucy A. Sames' work with Res. articulated in their doctoral thesis *Wet Rest: excess as liquid praxis in art and curating* (2022) and in their collaborative book *Alembic* (Jury et al. 2018).

4 Here, speaking explicitly in the context of Palestine and the urgency of action to demand an end to Israeli violence against Palestinians.

7 Bric-à-brac and the Artist-Run

[IMT] is definitely rhizomatic, it's not a tree structure. Also […]
really putting out like doubts about the world and insecurities,
like 'we don't know how we do this but we go along', [unlike
the] direct […] clarity [of a] power centre. […] It's really organic,
or like an organism, it's not just like a straight business plan.
(Kjær Skau 2021, personal communication, 21 December)

Cooke describes this organic unknowing as a contingency:

I wanted to work with the gallery because of this contingency,
there's always contingency in the way that we operate that
opens up the ability for something to drastically change and
for us not to have complete control over the output, and I think
that's exciting and I think that's important in terms of audience
encounter.
(Cooke 2021, personal communication, 2 December)

Similarly, Charles Danby, an artist and curator, who has, on
different occasions, performed both roles at IMT suggests, for
him, it is about having access to modelling:

Bruce High Quality Foundation, [prior to their involvement
in the IMT exhibition *Epilogues: It Started with a Car Crash*
(2011), were] touring across America, opening up spaces into
other modellings of art schools, which became another facet of
the dispersed work [of the exhibition], beyond the IMT borders
in conjunction with the Woburn Square Research Space at

DOI: 10.4324/9781003197959-8

UCL. All those things were strategies to work across, dissolve and disperse structural boundaries and borders. Working with IMT enabled mobilizations around these points [of dispersal]: rethinking and thinking through exhibition structures: what they *can* be, what their transformations are, what their positions are. And to come back to the core of IMT, this is a counter-institutional modelling. That's the most fundamental thing. And the momentum for me, the aggregation, the interest in somewhere like IMT as an independent curator.

(Danby 2022, personal communication, 13 January)

Slager, in their essay 'Academy as Exhibition', describes concerns that stem from an emergence in the 1990s of artistic research (re: academe) and how 'forms of resistance could emerge against the powers that discipline artistic knowledge' (Slager 2015:85).[1] Slager asks, in terms of the models of research defined by institutions:

Can we chart moments of deconstruction and de-territorialisation, moments of resistance to the managerial domain and moments of refusal of instrumental reason? Does the current society of spectacles, the world of marketing and commodity, actually allow an outside?

(ibid. 84)

Danby's view is that IMT is a counter-institutional modelling. The institution if it is anything is something with structure, consistency, and longevity. IMT may have some of these, but they are necessary weak points that can be moulded and adapted in ways that the institution proper resists. What Danby's view of IMT suggests is crucial. The unsettledness of IMT, our refusal to be articulated within a set domain, suggests a space that supports different subjectivities and agendas rather than demands conformity within its operations into a specific required order. This offer of counter-institutional modelling can be supportive of difference, of multi-plicity and of polyphony.[2] Such support is clearly essential for the sustaining of a Third Mind.

How does a counter-institutional space structure itself? The gallery is made up of roles; smaller galleries are often named after their director. We, the small group of people, the deciders, must name ourselves. Not part of the trajectory and instrumentalization of the curatorial in Higher Education, our relationship to the roles we adopted at the formation of IMT is empirical and practice based. Yet our roles appear decisive, instituted, drawn from a handbook rather than a bestiary: director; curator. Yet even in this tiresome rigidity the reality of these roles is that they are in a constant state of coming into being. For a gallery of our size and in its unsettled remodelling, responsibilities are not fixed. In small organizations like art galleries (especially those the size of IMT) employee payroll is kept at a minimum. In Magnus Resch's bible of art neoliberalism *Management of Art Galleries*, his survey claims that 6% of galleries in the UK are one person (rising to 11% if taking the United States and Germany into account). After that, most employees for a gallery will be part-time with over 60% of art galleries in the UK employing fewer than five part-time or full-time personnel (Resch 2018:37). Given this and the low turnover of small galleries, staff roles need to be both porous and versatile. Even the most common out-sourced roles in art management: technicians and art handlers (for the transportation of artworks 'nail to nail'), might on occasion be out of budget, requiring technical skills and driving licences drawn from the available team. This versatility and porousness has significant impact on concepts of authorship, a value entrenched in the history of art, especially in its commerce. Although I was the curator, IMT's first exhibition had already been determined by Friend.[3] My role then was as technician and the main contributor of voice: press releases, talks, narratives of funding bids. Over time some of these roles have shifted: Friend and others now contribute significantly more voice for some aspects of IMT's work. Much of this fluctuation happens because time is a resource and our capacity to spend time on IMT has also shifted. Some projects have a less than clear curatorial authorship, often unclear even to us. This is counter-institutional and follows the conception of IMT as a multiplicity holding itself together. Such authorship (at the level of the gallery's overall structure as well as exhibition-making), an authorship of multiplicity, encourages alternative infrastructures and logic systems. And to risk evoking the neoliberal Lovecraftianism of an organization being an organism (itself also an unavoidable implication of artist-as-business), IMT is always in the process of becoming-gallery, rather than being a gallery. As above so below.

Since working with Plastique Fantastique, Friend and I have begun more and more to view what IMT does as somehow representative of the terminology of fictioning as Burrows and O'Sullivan describe it, linking what Plastique Fantastique does through performance, via John Russell, D&G, and Foucault, as enunciations that mark 'roles or positions within a number of discursive regimes [or that can] mutate or traverse more than one structure or regime' (2019:5). This seems more mobile than how Suzana Milevska differentiates the becoming-curator from becoming a curator in (2013:65–71), explicitly as a negotiation 'of the discursive constitution of subject' (ibid. 66), but still maintains the curatorial as enunciative. So, our being (as *personnel*) become less about titles and more an intertwining through enunciations, 'intertwining the construction of subjectivity with that of institutions' (ibid. 70).

For many small galleries this kind of porousness is a necessity. But it also reflects what Phillips identifies as the realities of collaboration in contemporary art projects, that are not just as declared in collaborative authorship but are visible in labour that is also technical, administrative, managerial, supportive, economic, and domestic (Phillips 2019:303). What this analysis contests is the legitimacy of the tendency of an audience to follow particular 'miraculous' connections in the narrative of production that usually, though not always, chooses the artist as the common connection in a series of work, rather than such players as a gallery manager, technician, or financier which, as Stephen Knott argues in his critique of specialism, 'obfuscates the inherently collaborative and consensual dynamics that underpin highly skilled production' (Knott in Blamey 2016:73).

For IMT as a curatorial practice (and it should be understood by now that this is a subjective reading of IMT as an entity, rather than an objective reading of part of IMT as a builder of exhibitions) this porousness is a methodology. It works both at the level of personnel and the level of the gallery-as-organization (although it should also be clear that there is no clear distinction where these two terms meet).

Firstly, and synthetically, then: the organization. The gallery, as the title of this book suggests, is a hybrid space. The hybrid has important precedents in understanding the organization of alternative and artist-run art galleries, going back to Batia Sharon's 1979 text 'Artist-run galleries', which argues that such spaces arise from an inability to access existing commercial platforms. By extending this into the institutional, artist-run galleries often seem to arise from the realization that Fine Art degrees often don't translate into a sustainable Fine Art practice. Although Fine Art degrees do often attempt to reveal structures and practices of the industry, including its reliance on wealth, power, and closed social factions, this seems in cruel contrast to energies of creative liberation spoken about in studio practice, yet clearly part of the ecosystem that students are guided towards by this education.

Finding ourselves in London at the beginning of the 21st century, confused about how to conciliate the radical promise of ideas and the art school with the alienating movement of art though art markets, we try and understand, through practice, how both could exist. And if neither existed, then what might remain. When IMT was founded in 2005, the idea that art in and of itself could solve problems through its existence was more widespread than now, where art's failings (or rather the critique of art's social function) was less widespread than it is now. In IMT's case, and embedded in its founding documents from 2005, is the conviction that the existence of contemporary art itself can be for the public good. So, we start with a gallery that was a hybrid of worlds and curated it as a means of either finding answers or pushing gallery practice to points at which it fails. As such, IMT is a hybrid space in that it adopts characteristics of models drawn from both the commercial gallery sector (exclusive representation of artists and participation in art fairs), characteristics normally associated with artist-led or garage spaces (non-profit company structure and projects funded through public bodies) as well as characteristics reminiscent of affiliation with academic teaching and research.

In their discussion of the various categories of curator, Adrian George attempts differentiation between the concerns of the artist and those of the curator, especially where they are at their messiest in the complex category of artist-curator. They link the rise of the artist-curator to Joshua Reynolds, then El Lissitzky, before making a clear statement around what artist-curators are. For George they are artists *as* curators. This is not an entirely satisfactory definition, but useful in imagining the idea of an artist-run gallery. They say that:

> many additional elements of curatorial practice [beyond] the display of works of art [...] such as programme planning,

administration, fundraising, writing interpretation, marketing, press, personnel and building management – may not be something an artist wants, or is equipped to do.

(George 2015:8)

Cooke's articulation of curator-artist relationships is useful here. Cooke is an artist-curator, already a hybrid form that rejects the separation of curator from artist especially in its foregrounding of artist in that formulation. Like Friend and I, Cooke had come from a Fine Art background:

so [I] look at mediation critically as a conceptual and material expression in itself but one that is largely not articulated in exhibition practice. Therefore, mediation becomes a site for experimentation in which it can be rendered tangible; through staging the discussions with the artistic practices.

(Cooke 2022, personal communication, 28 September)

In this formulation this is a means of remaining visible, not to claim space but to acknowledge their existence in the environment of the work (the gallery exhibition), a position that has traces from the 1960s in which role of curator began to be understood as authorial in terms of the *act* of exhibition-making (see, for example, O'Neill 2012).

The artist Lotte Rose Kjær Skau, who is also a programme director at LungA School, describes it thus:

I guess it's this complete blurriness of being in a mode where everything that's happening, the life you're living, is an art practice. But not as something else in your life. And it's not about being aware and boringly thinking heavily about everything you do, but it's really about the *presence* in what you do. If you're present yourself you realise just what objects around you are really present. It's about being really attentive to when the work you are part of becomes free. [At LungA] because they had to do everything they got a deep understanding. They had to embrace sweeping the floor as an artistic practice. And sometimes when we start the programme and we need some walls built then we start doing it together because that's a great way to know each other. It would be way easier for us to build the walls ourselves. We know how to do it. So it's not the easy choice. But have the participants become a part of this doing. When putting up exhibitions it's not about how you now get an exhibition curated by us, it's about who ... we just make up these things together that just create something. Staying with the trouble sometimes.

(Kjær Skau 2021, personal communication, 21 December)

This role of the artist-turned-curator is possible partly due to the increased shapelessness of both expectations of artistic expansion outside of disciplines and departments as well as the unregulated art sector in the UK. In *The Culture of Curating and the Curating of Culture(s)*, O'Neill describes how the figure of the curator of art slides into view as an auteur figure of the exhibition-as-form, partly through the effort of artists to want to demystify the process by which exhibitions are made. My curatorial role at IMT, and my role as the primary author of this account, is indicative to some degree of this rise and reveal of the curator. As curators start to become visible actors in how exhibitions are made and how art is itself given visibility, the role of the curator has become something that artists can find intrusive, manipulative, unethical, or larcenous. I learnt about curating primarily from practice as well as from conversations with artists and curators, anecdote, rumour, and gossip being a key text. This was not uncommon, and Gavin Butt's analysis of the importance of gossip amongst cultural workers for a real understanding of art history testifies to its efficacy (Butt 2005).

This shapelessness, and conversational mode of engaging with art-making and exhibition-making informs my curatorial practice, and the earlier examples *AAS: The Cult of Possible Elements* (2014) and *This Is a Not-Me* (2020) make this methodology the material conditions of how the work becomes made.

Being an artist-run space suggests a specific mode of activity: one that is creative. Creativity suggests alternative positioning that seeks not to replicate the old, the status-quo, but to manifest something *new*. Sharon identifies that artist-run spaces seem to rise from the organization of 19th-century groups the *Salon des Réfusés* and the *Salon des Indépendants*, yet states that the artist-run is far broader than the avant-garde and includes a considerable number of more traditional spaces (Sharon 1979:5–14). As such, artist-run spaces are often viewed from a particular, and often unfair, self-promotional lens.

IMT does not often describe itself as an artist-run space, and not for this reason. Our avoidance of this term, for ourselves, was about stepping into otherness. I'd tried and failed to make being an artist a default mode, working through other systems from this perspective, and Friend and I were keen to understand what it looked like from the position of those for whom the default language was the business of organization. This is not to say that artists are unable to engage with such systems, but that the artist-run space seems to separate the hybrid into two. The worker in the hybrid gallery is protean, and the gallery doesn't hold its pattern (keeping its inconsistencies somehow together) if their form were to become more settled. As such, such spaces can tend to fall apart if becoming aligned to more restrictive infrastructures. The artist somehow has a career outside of the space, whereas for Friend, they are the same hybrid creature. We therefore resist describing IMT as an artist-run gallery, but to reprise Friend's articulation and acknowledge the primacy of the Third Mind: IMT is an artist-as-gallery. It should be clear that the artist-run being discussed here is one that, through ideological creativity, is explicitly an unsettling. We are unsettled, and not just in the context of a fixed mode of activity, or as a variable, or something precarious, although we are all these things, but also in the sense of being unsettled that is ill at ease, a discomfort, an anxiety.

For me there was already a precedent in a structure to work through hybrid arrangements. In 2002, the artist Henrik Schrat, then a fellow MA student at the Slade School of Fine Art, invited a bank manager into the Slade as a manager in residence: *Manager in Residence (MiR)* (2002). At the time the successful applicant, Dominic Palfreyman, worked in investment banking at Goldman Sachs and Deutsche Bank and had previously been managing director of WestLB in London, and was interested in 'the business of being an artist, the use and abuse of art by business, and those artists that take business as a subject matter' (Schrat 2002). In a letter to *Art Monthly*, in response to Peter Suchin's criticism of the work as an example of 'campus capitalism' (Suchin 2002), Schrat clarified that, for him, 'the challenge for the artist is to learn about economic and corporate structures, and to come of age culturally by doing so and so becoming able to confront the corporate world from a position of knowledge'. For Schrat 'familiar ideo-logical superstructures [...] are not only inefficient, but they also hamper development and become dangerous, reproducing the very power structure they claim to do away with'. He proposes instead to 'claim the economy and the circulation of money as cultural positions and establish critique from within the system' (Schrat 2003). I had never read Henrik's proposition as a means of moving artists and arts education further towards capital, as Suchin feared, but instead that the discordance between the two systems would make a third that might produce interesting effects. I saw them as two diagrams placed over one another, out of sync but revealing discordances in the conflicts and synergies of their individual dynamics.[4]

Friend's approach was similar. She wasn't concerned in which system a gallery was located, but what its practices could afford us. Sansone Ruiz:

> The curatorial practice of IMT is much more about curating *what IMT is*. Lindsay was in the period of reinvention and exploration, going to art fairs, putting money in places where she hadn't put it. Like she studied [other galleries, non-profit, commercial and institutions], and she got these incredible observations, thinking about models and different ways of making something that was sustainable. [The] key [for artists and young arts organisations] would be learning about different economic models. Everything from like cooperative economics. Students are passionate about art, they know about art, they're going to think about art, that stuff is the easy part, it's about investing the time in learning history, theory, and mechanics of different economic models.
>
> (Sansone Ruiz 2021, personal communication, 12 October)

Given that IMT co-opts models from the commercial sector as part of its creativity, claims that art galleries are for the public good is more challenging to land than, for example, Wade's claim for artist-run spaces such as Eastside Projects. Morgan Quaintance argues this dichotomy in his review of the 2015 Turner Prize. He maintains that although 'contemporary art is a critically engaged field that, for the most part, produces crit-ically engaged actors who are uncomfortable with state power and its various methods of citizen subjection', art galleries now are 'structured and funded to serve the interests of Capital and the state' (Quaintance 2015). Certainly, without public funding, this will necessarily need to be the case. In fact, IMT's hybridity between a space supportive of garage-style artist-led, publicly funded arts exhibitions and a commercial model of representing artists and pursuing commission on artist sales became explicit with a major change in the accessibility of public funding. This change was in 2010 when, under pressure from the government, the Arts Council England restricted its funding application process so that funded projects had to be complete before a new application could be submitted. Prior to this IMT had functioned on a series of rolling applications, allowing a year-long programme of Arts Council funded projects, without having to make an application for a programme. Part of our work as gallerists was to be the authors of funding applications, absolving artists of the majority of that labour. The benefit of this was that where project funding failed, the gallery could still survive with the projects that succeeded rather than relying on a single application for a year's funding. Friend and I were already subsidizing IMT through drawing no salary and taking on other jobs, Friend able to support this position through also being an arts administrator whilst I had, from 2008, started teaching as an associate lecturer. But if IMT was to also exist outside of regular public funding, it would need a significant source of alternative income.

A key factor in IMT's founding in 2005 had been its constitution as a company, a move that seemed so important it nearly emptied a tiny account that had been used as the business account for Space TwoTenTwo (see Chapter 11). Friend recalls: 'We had £100 in the account which was transferred from Space TwoTenTwo. £85 of this went into incorporating as a company, a non-profit limited by guarantee'. Such a decision places IMT in a position favoured by many funding bodies as well as on a trajectory to become a charity; however, Friend made a firm statement that the latter wouldn't be an aim for IMT as she didn't want to risk her autonomy.

In their brief distillation of UK, German and US art gallery economics, Resch (2018) devises a three-tier trading structure for gallery operation, directed at the market: garage, gallery, and fine art. These are of course structures that already exist, but

Resch's intention is that they be considered as structures under the umbrella of a single gallery. As extant structures, it should be clear from the previous chapter that the garage is the structure from which IMT has grown: an organization 'from the non-profit model of a Kunsthalle [motivated by] community spirit and the desire to see exhibiting success among the artist group [and] supported by a small ground of benefactors, which includes the gallery owner' (ibid. 60). However, it is also evident that IMT operates in the second 'gallery' tier: representing a small group of core artists (ibid. 61).

Resch calls for a move from art historical specialization to art market specialization, a move that may solve Quaintance's dichotomy by removing the critical engagement from its interference in the interests of capital. Resch correctly identifies that garage spaces do not make profit but instead trade in cultural capital and 'credibility'.[5] Whilst the big profits are to be found in the third tier: trading in the secondary market. A proposal for the art market outlines the problem: currently commercial galleries dealing in both the primary and secondary market are doing so on a bedrock of earnest labour by garage galleries. Resch's neoliberal solution is to combine these activities within a single organization. On the one hand it might be assumed that this is exactly what is meant by the concept of a gallery as hybrid. There are galleries that operate successfully on precisely this basis, the example most familiar to me being Workplace Gallery/Workplace Foundation in London/Gateshead. However, this is not what I mean. Workplace's structure is clearly divided and operates strategically and systematically to support the tiers it is responsible for. It is difficult to argue that we do not have an appetite for such things as sustainability (personal as well as organizational) and, as per Eastside Projects, of surviving in a capitalist economy, although surviving is not the same as being settled. But as each strategy for accomplishing this begins to complete, we find ourselves short-circuiting it, being internecine, refusing a particular mode of performing into a system or jumping suddenly from one system's conventions into another, remaining fugitive; unsettled. This is an ethical refusal that pulls us back and forth across an uncanny threshold. There are clear synergies with the becoming of Delueze, in a comparable state of change, of not being fixed, and also the terms of a smudging of basic communication formula after Burroughs, and it comes partly from a need to do things, as much as possible, on our own terms, as well as moments of fear and anxiety.

IMT appeared and matured at a time when critical and commercial activities in the arts exhibited an awkward coexistence. In his bleak assessment of the university and the creative industries, Raunig identifies within the early 2000s 'the term *creative industries* [becoming] successively established through Europe in cultural policy programs' with a shift in state funding from critical to commercial enterprise (2013:112). This was clear in the UK when the Arts Council England moved to prioritize funding to organizations that could also demonstrate sustainability, whether by operating successfully within art markets or by providing paid-for services to artists and creatives. These services most commonly involved subsidizing a gallery by acting as landlords for hire of exhibition space, rehearsal spaces, studio, or hot desk space. However, this concept of supporting only projects that are financially sustainable prioritizes a relationship to the money nexus that not only precedes social value but also risks overlooking those who demand the primacy of social value.

Speaking at the *Contemporary Arts Research Forum: Experiment Now*, (Northumbria University 3 May 2022) about their work running non-profit curatorial collective Lungs Project, one of its founders Sheyda Aisha Khaymaz stresses, 'We are not a viable business. This is not a business model'. Whilst they might be right, projects like Lungs are no less important regardless of their viability as a business, and there are many easy arguments for it being a business model. For one it performs an urgent role supporting up-and-coming practices, from, in their terms, 'chronically underrepresented backgrounds' (Lungs Project 2022). It is, perhaps, a function of contemporary business that such work is, or becomes, by its very nature unviable. That support for the underrepresented, marginalized, and erased, addressing inequalities of visibility and power, is a work of ethics, not of profits. So Khaymaz's statement about not being viable is not an admission of failure but an assertion of the very importance and long-term urgency of the work Lungs Project is doing. Indeed, it could be that Lungs' unviability is part of its ability to foreground its activism and be able to remain urgent in how it responds ethically and decisively to support the artists and writers that it does. Likewise, Sasha Burkhanova-Khabadze on Exposed Arts Projects:

What do [we] mean by sustainable? Something that's capable of going on from year to year with some predictability and stability? We feel unsure about the future and [have] financial insecurity, but at the same time we have this growing pot of people who get what we do and see how it benefits and they come back and then help us.

(Burkhanova-Khabadze in Tomlinson 2021:21)

Artists are often in an employment entirely unrelated to their valued practices, and so might be more able to imagine financial failure in the same breath as professional success, but it is also evidently about maintaining tension between social ethics and the money nexus.

IMT's founding comes from an idealism: primary refusal of the money nexus as guiding force and thus IMT's existence not as a business to make money, but as a multi-authored resource for artists and visitors. We wanted to work with art that wasn't alienating, that wasn't integrated into the money nexus, into corporate production or the collection ritual. We referred to this internally at IMT as work that 'resists commodification'. In many ways this seems to place IMT within consensus with orthodoxy. If we, as I do in this book, place the curatorial at the heart of IMT's concerns then the separation of curating from commerce is a somewhat mainstream position in contemporary practice. Obrist's *Ways of Curating* speaks of how 'curating follows art' (2014:24) and lists the functions of curating as preservation, selection, historicization (specifically the making of art history), and exhibition-making. These are convenient if somewhat idealistic in that they easily allow the reader to evoke a curating exterior to the cash nexus that gives each of these functions its mass. Contrast this idealism to Ziherl who describes the curator instead as 'among those who moderate [the] form-giving process [of] differing ideals of art, [curated by and pursued by capital]' (2016:225). As such, for Ziherl, the art that Obrist's curator follows and how they select what to curate conforms to capital's ideals. For Ziherl this moderation is through pragmatism. Ziherl's text is an important and urgent demand for addressing imbalances in control and autonomy in the curatorial act, and in demanding accountability. Their formulation of the curator as moderator under the influence of the ideals of capital is an important one as it forms the foundations of inequity. The moderator maintains the status quo by filtering out alterity, and any resistances to the smooth flow of capital, whatever, or whoever, they may be. This was something IMT sought to resist even as endemic as it is within art world infrastructures.

To borrow a model of relations from Serres (1982), art, in an art world, is a cascade of parasites. Something is produced and a series of parasites make their meals from it. The artist's share can be meagre unless the system is formalized, whereupon they may receive around half, but what's often ignored is that the artist is a parasite too. Their work is less and less a production as Serres describes production. It isn't the butter churn. It is, more and more, a conversation with things and with itself. An image of a butter churn. It is like a candy, reminiscent of something, a taste of something, imagined, processed, and shared. Art, a meal that is a candy, in an art world, a home that is an industry that 'pillages and plunders' (1982:3). Charles Esche agrees as much, saying 'an individual curatorial practice [is] a parasitical activity in the end', where a curator's skill lies in ensuring 'that something approximating a curatorial vision remains visible through the tangle of financial and other interests' (Esche in Martinon 2013:241).

Here the curator seeks, perhaps for their own professional preservation or their pride, to remain visible as a project translates into a public and moves within the world.

This is, Esche says, the clever curator. Such a curator may be undone by the messiness of the hybrid were it to be revealed in all its hulked life but, as Esche says, the curatorial position is compromised by money, power and organization (ibid. 242) and IMT does not escape even though it might want to.

There are many people living inside.

Ziherl also correctly attaches the curatorial to something that IMT is currently unable to repudiate, and that I have previously discussed: 'conventionally curatorial authorship is read towards architecture in a bricks-and-mortar sense' (2016:7), an attachment that reinforces the role of urban infrastructure and planning in the maintenance of capitalism, and an additional dynamic to capital's control and moderation. What are our solutions? As others have pointed out, the instrumentalization of alterity can also carry with it and further imbed these imbalances (Quaintance 2020a and 2021, Hylton 2007 and de Mille in ICA 2016). For de Mille, for example, organizations often use alterity as a means to trade, but asymmetrically, the rewards not distributed fairly or evenly. Beech argues for amateurism and incompetence, which display 'critical promise within modern and avant-garde art because they shake the hegemony of what has been authorised' (2010:53). This is clearly part of IMT's unsettled methodology, however since Beech's text the increased visibility and pervasiveness of #MeToo disclosures and Black Lives Matter has made amateurism and incompetence a concern that relies, as does the fair distribution of rewards, on the ethical commitment of the amateur and the incompetent.

Black Swan also identifies a key deficit: 'The people that give in the art world are generally the project spaces, the offsites, the lower-tier galleries, the digital critical platforms and the unpaid curators' (2022a:281) and it is clear that the phrase 'support artists' is a description of an act of giving. At its most generous the commercial model extracts from collectors to support artists and gallery, whereas the non-profit model extracts from funders to support artists, gallery, and audiences. But in both cases, where resources are poor and desperation high, there is evident risk of parasitism, despite any intention of the act of giving: the exploitation of artists' labour (and paying for this labour is hardly an act of giving), as well as that of gallerists, and competing over intellectual property. In the years we've been running we've seen established galleries keeping money from artists to gamble on art fairs (and losing); artists embezzling funds raised for exhibitions; major, wealthy collectors trying to make artists break agreements with their galleries in order to save money on buying the work; major institutions ignoring copyright to publish work we commissioned; galleries damaging work and refusing to pay for it on their insurance. These are the products representative of a corrupt and unregulated industry. They remain because there is a fear of losing capital (financial or cultural) on resisting them.

Friend became interested in representation to be part of the labour involved in an artist's means to trade. One of the first practices she put in place was something rare for art galleries: a formal contract. Whereas most galleries at that time (and still) rely on the informality of a handshake we were seeing artists we were working with routinely disenfranchised by this gesture by galleries who claimed to represent or otherwise support them: artworks would go missing or be held to ransom, artists unpaid for sales and exhibition promises rescinded. When stars die, they become voids that suck everything in.

Within the experimental remit of IMT, representation offered experiments with how the money nexus impacts on art and the lives of artists. And we felt that representation could be more horizontal.

In conversation with Burrows we talked about what the gallery might be about, he described it in terms of his work with Plastique Fantastique:

> A good friend once said, 'Plastique Fantastique can be excruciating, but then there'll be a moment and it will be transformative and amazing'. And I think that I'm always interested in that moment, which might not happen for everybody at the same time, but you're caught and you're in it and there's no longer any distance between you and what's happening and because it's a communal thing you think everyone feels the same, and you feel it amplified because you sense maybe other people are there with you. And that's why art that obliterates interests me. And I think that's what Plastique Fantastique does. *That's* the relation that I'm interested in.
>
> Part of doing Plastique Fantastique is it's a collaboration, so people come together and even if they only do it once I hope they get something out of it. And the nicest moments when we've either done it, or about to do it, and spent time together, and that's important too. And maybe that's what the gallery's about, having something that's your own. Having your own autonomy and it's removed from other kinds of purposes.
>
> (Burrows 2021, personal communication, 26 October)

One of the things our own autonomy is about is refusing something even as we deploy it, like the trickster organization provoking ridicule and bringing discredit upon ourselves. And so here is where I need to depart from a certain type of describing in order to think. Because the hybrid is not just a hybrid of artist-run, non-profit, commercial, and pedagogic. The hybrid, meanwhile, in the way it's to be intended here, does not think quite as clearly. The hybrid, for example, is not strategic but tactical. The hybrid is an unsettled plan of living. It is like a vortex, there are no resting points (Serres

1977). What other kinds of purposes might it be removed from? The income of the salaryman? The seriousness of businessmen? The art world itself, as an entity defined by a lack?

The idea that the making-public of art be organized as a business and conform, for example, to Mark Fisher's 'business ontology' (2009:17) and the urge to resist this model (whether artistic instinct for a-causality or a learned part of the culture of the avant-garde) is at the heart of the hybrid. A hybrid, at any moment, is in transition from being one thing to another, an egg on a tongue. It is an ontological paradox. To exist in relation to the structures it hybridizes it must be woven from a different logic. As such it is its own diagram – like Schrat's *MiR*, the hybrid is the diagrammatic overlaying of the business ontology matrix and the other matrices that may need to be defined amongst movements for creativity. There are histories of magic(k) here, especially those histories that later managed to escape their domination by characters like Burroughs and Crowley and to become reunited with non-white non-cis male, revolutionary power.[6] This seems to mimic Cooke's concerns with Easterling and Mignolo. However, Cooke's strategy also sees this issue as one tied up with image itself:

> My approach to art and, I think, the approach IMT has, is drawn from *The Graven Image* by Zainab Bahrani and how she critiques history. [...] She highlights that the Western interpretation of art can only be a representation, it can only be mimicry.
> (Cooke 2022, personal communication, 28 September)

In Bahrani this starts from the singular god of monotheism, what in Burroughs might be described as the OGU (the One God Universe). For Bahrani, the king is semi-divine and therefore any image of the king is merely a copy or a mimic; it cannot be the thing itself. In Assyrian and Babylonian culture however, there is the practice of salmu, a culture of text, image, and ritual. Cooke sees this in terms of it being a diagram that then 'becomes ritualised through these performances or the encounter' a term Cooke uses often as a means of centring exhibition-making on encountering, and then in Bahrani's terms it is '*through that* the image; [a painting, a sculpture, a person;] can become the king' (ibid.). Bahrani's analysis is concerned with rewriting the way that polytheist cultures and artefacts have been fundamentally misunderstood by the West, whose own logic system can't recognize how gods are written. With the West spreading its logic system through modernity and capitalism, it has spread what is quite a restrictive lens, and one that perpetuates the same way of looking at the world. However, in Cooke's following of Bahrani and adaption of this analysis into their work on the encounter, Bahrani's analysis changes the stakes for artworks that are no longer representations of kings but can be written as kings: and, therefore, art, and art-as-fictioning, has a stake in the Real.

In Burroughs' meaning of art, he places it very much outside the OGU and instead within a polytheist dynamic (even if a mythical one viewed obsessively from a Western lens of hedonistic libertarianism). For Burroughs, art is 'magical in origin' and in 'making things happen' (1986a:60), a similar stake in the Real that Cooke calls for via Bahrani. It is also an art that brings the *spontaneous generation* that precedes the Enlightenment and the arrival of plagues that normally come from Gods: 'Dogs leap out of a picture [...] typus lice concealed in the bindings' (Burroughs 1986a:63). A virus comes off the page – it is a good to talk about methodology – the virus enters the viewer via the encounter to make them rewire their mode of thinking or operating within these normative conditions. The COVID-19 pandemic has made this explicit: the alien tongue carries a virus. Alien saliva caries a virus. The candy on the tongue, the candy on the floor, carries a virus. The brain. The tongue. The egg. So, it leaks up and enters you and makes you reconfigure your relationship to the environment.

Allow me to change register.

Notes

1 Slager's example is the first Tbilisi Triennial in 2012.
2 Other galleries have articulated comparable approaches, for example, Sarah Jury, Helen Kaplinsky and Lucy A. Sames' Res. project, which ran from 2015 to 2018 in Deptford. Similarly to the unsettled characteristic of IMT, Res. claimed to be 'mutable'. Helen Hester articulates a positionality that has comparable claims as these, oriented through a form of feminist poshumanism they refer to as xenofeminism, both in *Xenofeminism* (2018), drawing on feminist 'radical amateurism' and its emancipatory role, and in condensed form in their essay 'n Hypotheses of Post-Cyber Feminism' in Res.'s *Alembic* (Jury et al. 2018:118–31).

3 *My Little Girl* (2005) by O Zhang, a photography graduate from Guangzhou, China, who now lives and works in New York.

4 Schrat would exhibit at IMT in *Report on Probability B* (2012), a 'revisiting of Modernism under the aegis of a Science Fiction narrative' (IMT 2012).

5 Even where garage spaces are aware of how they are exploited, it is difficult to defend oneself. From our own experience, some powerful commercial galleries connected to collectors eager to get a deal will happily ignore existing contracts between artists and spaces like IMT and petition these artists to sell work out of their studio.

6 John Cussans' work on the 'zombie complex' and his charting of movements of the zombi from the Haitian revolution is of particular force here (2017).

8 All Money Is Blood[1]

The 1989 board game *Space Hulk* designed by Richard Halliwell for Games Workshop is set in the Warhammer 40k universe. In that universe a 'space hulk' is a postmodern collection of architectural structures ripped apart by mystical forces of entropy and chaos and forced back together again to form new permutations, like a cut-up or a fold-in. Within the *Space Hulk* bestiary there are also hybrids. The hybrid in *Space Hulk* emerges from a metamodelization of mechanics, lore and commerce just as much as IMT does, so let me play the comparison out.

Space Hulk was inspired by the success of the movie *Aliens* (1986) but which also drew directly from the pages of *2000 AD*, a British comic that delivered thinly veiled anti-fascist, anti-authoritarian and anti-Thatcher politics to children in the 1970s and 1980s. In *Space Hulk* one player plays a squad or squads of fascist, techno-theist humans (the 'Imperium of Man'), whilst the other plays waves of alien creatures that assault them inside a hulk. The hulks were formally separate vessels that merge by appearing into the material universe at the same time and space as one another, exiting from an alternate dimension of pure psychic energy ('The Warp'). According to Uma Breakdown, who deploys 40k law as a key text in their practice, The Warp is comparable to 'the Deleuzo-Guattarian plane of immanence – a plane of potential, anticipation, possibilities and energy, and "an infinite multiplicity of different types of becomings"' (Breakdown in Sames 2022:98).[2] The game itself reflects this in the collision of lore and mechanics: The lore impacts on the gaming environment by allowing players to build space craft that make no reasonable

DOI: 10.4324/9781003197959-9

sense, but instead appear and disappear with the requirements of individual games. This is a game. A creature that appears.

The alien menace is at home in these techno-architectural hybrids, the marines seek to 'cleanse' them. This dynamic (that of alien menace versus human marines, known in the game as 'Terminators', another folded movie reference) is a colonialist trope of a tribal, barbarous Other versus righteous technology/ civilization, not uncommon in games from 'Cowboys and Indians' to the post-2010 proliferation of board game versions the post-Romero iteration of the zombie myth.[3] *Space Hulk*, as a Games Workshop property, has a more politically aware moral register. It is not just the hulks themselves that are hybrids, in fact these are not the hybrids I'm evoking here. The hulks are different technologies from different universes somehow caught in a holding that keeps them consistent – they may not work in terms of their original design, but they work as maps for conflict (the requirements of the game mechanics) as well as a means to make the alien menace an existential threat to humanity (the requirements of the lore). Within the hulk live creatures in process of hybridizing. This process happens outside of the mechanics of the base game (exists in lore only), but is brought into game mechanics through the commercial interests of *Genestealer*, one of the two expansions for the game released in 1990. The game describes a hybridizing process of an insidious planting of an egg (delivered by tongue) from the alien to the human, in which generations of hybrid become 'more and more like their parent race and less and less like [the aliens, and that] tend to naturally band together into an extended "family" [with later generations] capable of understanding and using technology'. *Space Hulk: Missions & Background* (Halliwell 1989:23). The aliens impregnate the marines by licking them, in a reimagining of the thinly veiled subtexts of sexual violence and motherhood in the Alien franchise, to create new families. Once delivered, new hybrids are created, somewhere between the techno-fascist-theist Imperium of Man and the ungovernable otherness of expansive biological desire.

What happens in game terms is interesting for this discussion of IMT. The hybrids have lost the speed and the raw power of their inhuman claws, and neither do they have the toughness of the alien carapace nor the human armour. They have lost the versatility of the marines' command system and the extra actions of the purebred alien. But it also creates a new battle-field: a psychic battlefield conducted in some dimension (an idea space) at an angle to that in which the techno-collaged hulks float in the void.

The hybrid in *Space Hulk* is a new model, an act of 'conversion' or 'kit-bashing', an act of converting models away from the design, although in this new model we are provided with interchangeable arms and tools: human arms and alien arms on the same sprue. I don't know what a hybrid is when it is just a word, a trick of the first mouth, only when it is an object at hand that I can hold and pass around and see from all sides and bend it against its sprue and feel the flash to clean. I can inspect it, choose its colours and the order that they might be applied. I can imagine the new worlds, different to this one, that it may build. Worlds of subversive liber-ation that benefit from inconsistent technologies of representation (Hughes and Rohtmaa-Jackson 2022).

This is perhaps the best way I have found to describe what IMT might be as a hybrid object within the context of hybrid business models. A thing, notably aligned with the alien player, that is weakened by its techno-fascist-theist heritage but given range by it, and that, through its failed attempts to avoid the battlefield, is eager to create a new battlefield like a nested, matamodalized diagram.

The hybrid here is irrational in that it is unconcerned with the sound judgements of business practices. An inconsistent assemblage, its aetiology and morphology are Lovecraftian in their implausibility. It resists utility as it cannot be effectively instrumentalized (Ancelin-Bourguignon et al. 2019).

But *Space Hulk* is also an amalgamation of hybrids. As outlined, the hybrids inhabit hulks, themselves hybrids of lost spaceships fused together. But more so the theme itself is a hybrid of the zombie movie and the unidentified flying object (UFO): also hybrids. Zombies breach classifications: they are dead and alive; us and them; hungry and full; harmless and dan-gerous; slow moving and transient; loved ones who've suddenly turned into strangers (see, for example, Luckhurst 2015). UFOs are hybrids. They are:

> liminal and anti-structural; they are found betwixt and between the heavens and the earth (a binary opposition). They have

properties in common with angels, spirits, fairies, and demons. These are all interstitial, and when one enters this realm, one must tread cautiously because other binary oppositions can become blurred. The imagination-reality opposition is especially vulnerable.

(Hansen 2001:270)

If our hybrid is like a UFO, then they are a hybrid because they disturb the world in which they exist and, if they are viral, contributing to the blurring of binaries around them.

It may be a function of the hybrid gallery, and its reliance on affordance as a substitute for value, or as much a function of broader tactical (rather than strategic) arts activity under capitalism, that the work moves into every part of your life. Other specific factors contribute to this life–work amalgam, the social aspect of art world activity, and the deployment of every resource conceivable to maintain function. But from this position, it is difficult not to see everything as part of the project. That the hybrid is also holistic.

The hybrid (*Space Hulk*) evolves in lore but also in mechanics. The evolution of the hybrid has narrative purpose (in universe) that makes its evolution a success, yet it simultaneously (in game) conflicts with the simple and effective dualisms of the game's mechanics, the way that its actors function within the game come together and create a third way, less effective but revealing of apophatic characteristics. And this is ultimately because hybridity, as I have described it, is a creative force. Not because a hybrid gallery is run as an artist-run space but because it creates through cut-up, fold-in, and meta-modelization.

And obviously this book has a diagram laid over it, a diagram that may undo some of its logic, and may seem to short circuit some of its cause and effect and may perpetrate lies. But, maybe with faith in some swallowed magic, that will reveal truths like a letter cut into.

A candy was not meant to be a dying body.

Notes

1 A term Burrows used when describing working with galleries as a represented artists (2021, personal communication, 26 October).

2 Sames here referencing Breakdown's 2017 performance "*TFW: The Formless Wastes*" at Res. in London.

3 The launch of the popular reimagining of the comic *The Walking Dead* for television. Of the 1339 zombie-themed boardgames listed for publication from 1978 on boardgamegeek.com, 90% were released 2010 and later.

9   Death

Sansone Ruiz describes IMT's relationship to money: 'My favourite story about you guys was when [IMT was exhibiting] at the Manchester Contemporary[1] [and] you both started chanting "DEATH! DEATH! DEATH! DEATH!"' (Sansone Ruiz 2021, personal communication, 12 October). Money is the first mouth. Every taste is poison, every lick of the tongue deadening; every time it is written it becomes dead. And the gallery is as fragile as human bodies.

Sansone Ruiz messages me in May 2021 with a link to the *Bookforum* article 'Notes from the Cave: Searching for prophecy in the midst of a pandemic' by Joshua Cohen (2020). She messaged because William Burroughs is part of the story. This is the story of the fourth mouth. Cohen uses this story to draw connections, via Sontag, between Burroughs' account of language as virus and our current articulations of COVID-19. But the story also sits amongst my reveries on candy in its metaphoric ruminations of knowledge, death, and sucking. Sucking is not eating, it is not the ravenous consuming of the hungry, but a slow and leisurely act. But Cohen's sucking gives away something about language and knowledge: the sucking of Einstein's brain for knowledge makes your mouth numb. In Serres language is anaesthetizing (1985:310). 'Take time, remain silent, taste' (ibid. 157).

DEATH!

I struggle with the financial value of work. It makes me numb, reduces both complexity and movement to a dead presence. Death in the mouth. Not even a mouth anymore ... death in a hollow

DOI: 10.4324/9781003197959-10

where the mouth used to be. This slice of brain is poison. It is not the only thing in a jar, there is also an equally well preserved turd from Burroughs' plumbing[2] and they could easily be confused. Neither is meant to be eaten; it makes you gag. It is a bitter sliver that gets in the way of thinking about bodies and it numbs you and deprives you of language.

DEATH!

You cannot ignore the taste of death in a candy. We are raised to recognize in candy the taste of tooth decay and, more recently, the taste of obesity. The reminder of our bodies rotting into damp ashes and foul-smelling dust. But death is not the only episteme (Foucault) of the candy. Candy is also money. Candies are no longer made at home in their current state, they are born in the corner shop or the supermarket or the cinema.

DEATH!

In popular science fiction the candy is a neoliberal quasi-object. *The Happiness Patrol* (1988) uses candy as an instant gratification that is synthetic and temporary in a manner that denies the fullness of the human experience, and a vehicle for Thatcher-esq domination. Baudrillard (1976) explains the logic of the gift as something that has no equivalence. That it is a contrast to capitalism's value system of equivalence. A candy is a hybrid. It is a gift, but a gift utterly commodified by both weight and value. Or is this a mutation that is the epitome of ironical distance plus money fetishization that Fisher claims (via Zizek) to beat the heart of capitalist realism? (2009:13). In the future city of Judge Dredd, an amalgam of Thatcher-led urban policy in the UK, the candy has developed to the point that tastes so good it is highly addictive and thus outlawed.

DEATH!

The candy is a hybrid. The hybridity here is one that creates a tension between my own actions as a worker in the project and those conducted as a worker for the project. It should be clear that I did not go into this for the money, and, I suspect, neither did you. There is the chain of financial compensation which benefits artists we are working with before it benefits us, but that is not what I mean here. To move into art for the purposes of extracting money from its circulation is surely a deeply cynical one. Perhaps we might move into art because we see ourselves as able to perform a certain role in society. Perhaps because artists are, for whatever reason, given special consideration amongst human achievements. Perhaps because art is magic. But whatever the case, we are here. And it is likely not the financial value of the activity that keeps us here, but a belief in a power that is not about capital which makes me think that there is something alive in there. Clearly Roy Burns loves his child enough to kill to avenge his death. Can I justify, or properly articulate this thing that is not capital? The trajectory of the hybrid, as outlined, helps to define it. On the one hand we are interested in the rituals of exchange that are embedded in the art world and are interested to the point of destabilizing them. At the same time, these rituals offer real flows of cash that can be connected in a way that benefits artists. Resch's *How to Become a Successful Artist* is full of end-justifies-the-means. Lisa Schiff: 'Do whatever it takes to get your work out into the world' (Resch 2021:125); Mr Brainwash: 'Follow your dreams no matter what' (ibid. 152). These are demons trying to trick you into great evil. Remember, instead, the oft-shared Le Guin line from *Lathe of Heaven*: 'But what if there never is an end? All we have is means' (1971). Roy's love *precedes* his psychosis. There needs to be an assumption that the process of making this work public has a benefit before capital, as such that it has value that precedes any instance of financial exchange. This is the diagrammatic flow of our hybrid.

Commercial galleries seek to increase the value of the artwork through careful positioning of the work through a series of markets, collections, and other infrastructures. This is the art institution as factory (Fisher 2018:505–6, Steryll 2012:63 and Raunig 2013). For the art gallery, both its economic rational and its fundamental political positioning must be that the art is valuable for people. How people receive the benefit of this value is reliant on its structure. It may use its scant resources and networks to increase the value of works it has a stake in, receiving dividends as that work becomes centred by more visible institutions, but not without also using these resources and networks to make works available to audiences.

Given this, where does IMT's basic level of support come from? With major competition for public funds, a limit to how much we can channel from our salaries from outside of the gallery, and reluctance to become a factory, we still find ourselves looking for ways of co-opting from commercial approaches. Sansone Ruiz, who was co-curator at the gallery from 2014 to 2016 remembers it as a kind of performance:

> If I think back to those experiences now it was clearly experimenting with trying on various costumes, [asking] 'could IMT be a gallery that has rich collectors?' 'Could IMT be a gallery that has really swank private views?' [...] We experimented at that time with developing collectors, Lindsay was organising these nights with a couple of other galleries in the neighbourhood, [but it wasn't] to make more money [...] It was trying to accumulate more tools. It was just tools. It was trying to accumulate more tools to do more bonkers, like, absolutely out-of-this world stuff.
>
> (Sansone Ruiz 2021, personal communication, 12 October)

Here, Sansone Ruiz makes the tool-use of the hybrid explicit. The hybrid can take a tool from one sprue and activate it somewhere else. The tools are less effective in the hands of a hybrid, and the hybrid may often perform the production of value whilst not producing value, yet this is its out-of-this worldness, its alien malleability.

Nevertheless, hybridity needs a minimal consistency to exist. We may fear and yet be subservient to the rationality and influence of the market, a market that determines what art we hear about, teach, consume, and have access to be able to enjoy. And as such, in meagre resistance to this, we are drawn towards art we know will fail the test of marketization, that defies commodification. Something alien. A hybridity that, when managed perfectly, creates what Hansen describes as an anti-structure (Hansen 2001:178). But we need to feed the bodies hanging beneath our mouths, so we are on watch for opportunities to alchemically transform services, actions and cultural capital into alternatives to food.

Although less wealthy and established galleries are risking more by letting their resources circulate, at the same time they are opening possibilities through establishing generous networks from which they can borrow future resources that they don't hold themselves. Galleries without wealth who guard their resources closely will have significantly more limited options for display. If they struggle for funding and support emerging artists (who have had less time to amass their own equipment) then their exhibitions may become stale. Yet it is also tempting to think on how collaborations with others and sharing of resources seem more visible amongst the hybrid and garage galleries than the commercially robust. It is a socialism of sharing and support through scarcity where old projectors and screens circulate through exhibitions, rather than one of abundance of such resources where projectors stay more firmly in place. Sharing then becomes an aesthetic, just as wealth does. A certain curatorial device or technology that reveals your art world relations. A reel-to-reel tape recorder (*Trapped in a Sticky Shed with Side Chain Compression* [2019], a gift from the artist Stuart Tait), a red tape recorder (*Dead Fingers Talk* [2010], on loan from Elevator Gallery) a black tape recorder, the traces left by these circulating machines may not be explicit to all visitors, but are none the less detectable. Something familiar. A network of sucked candies carrying traces of other mouths, slipping away to sensation. The hybrid has more feelers, reaching into different biomes, so these aesthetics are potentially more varied: a display cabinet from Raven Row, a frame from the October Gallery, a projector from Sluice.

What is a gallery that either aims for or finds itself within a hybrid approach to organizing and processing art? Prior to fully embracing its hybrid status in 2011, it is worth tracing its more nascent phase from the prevailing cultural ecosystem of 2005 when IMT launched. Most galleries set up haphazardly are not, or would not want to be aiming for, the title of 'art institution'. Jonathan Harris instead uses the term 'formations', noting how the tendency of formations to be grouped around artistic movements (especially those of the Modernist avant-garde) have become led more by the ecosystem of production and consumption with little distinction 'between the 'institution' imposed from above and 'formation' created below' (Harris 2004:20). Resch inserts within this distinction the commercial and garage gallery ecosystem (2018) arguing an 'oversupply' of artists (and galleries) are competing for a comparatively small collection base. It is clear that collectors (i.e.

those willing to buy art) are much wider than Resch's grouping here, for Resch is describing art collectors in the most specialized sense, whereas we all, to some degree, have probably collected works made by individuals we'd consider artists, mostly in multiple form (DVDs or torrents of television shows, novels, comics, board games, video games, and even digital achievements within video games). We've also, I imagine, dabbled in uniques, whether signed photos from conventions or red carpets, Etsy objects or odd things picked up from strange places. It is not that there are too few art collectors but that there are too few collectors with access to the kinds of disposable income to spend on an object that might take someone weeks if not months to make without outsourcing art-making to underpaid assistants.[3]

Following Ziherl, Fisher, and others, organizing and presenting culture, by default, is an apparatus of existing power. The more one finds sustainable presence within an ecosystem such as the various art worlds that appear to sustain themselves, whether that is through sales or varying degrees of cultural capital, the harder it is to avoid this truth. Raicovich's investigation into cultural institutions suggests that even the neutrality of cultural institutions should be resisted in that they conceal 'the way in which power is wielded and maintained' (2021:141). This allows us instead to concentrate not on the simple observation of this, but to emphasize moments in which factors that contest power survive being part of this apparatus. It is clear that we need an origin story.

Notes

1 The Manchester Contemporary was an attempt to bring buying power outside of London. One of the founders Paulette Terry Brien describes its founding thus: 'In 2005 we realised that the art market plays a significant part in artists' development and that there wasn't really anyone working with artists in that way in Manchester' (Terry Brien in Bradbury 2013). The challenge of Manchester Contemporary was part of its allure for IMT as a hybrid, but as David Burrows put it after we performed there as Plastique Fantastique, Manchester Contemporary's hybridity is one of polar extremes: 'All art fairs are brutal, but Manchester is the most brutal because it's trying to mix up populism with also it being an art fair for elites' (Burrows 2021, personal communication, 26 October).

2 See *Words of Advice – William S. Burroughs on the Road* (2007), a documentary directed by Lars Movin and Steen Møller Rasmussen, screened at IMT in 2010 as part of *Dead Fingers Talk*.

3 Which, as Fisher points out, is a symptom of art-as-market anyway (2018:505).

10   A View from Elsewhere

It's 2004 and I am sitting on the toilet in Space TwoTenTwo. Friend is in the adjoining gallery office, which is also a living room. We are mythmaking, thinking of a name for a project space. I had, for some reason, left my copy of Barthes' *Image Music Text* here and I'm reading the back as something to do. It describes a desire; a desire to follow 'whatever turns, displaces, shifts, disperses' (1977).

I have the exact same copy of the book here now on my lap copying out the above. It is 2022 and I am in Gateshead, displaced by 18 years and nearly 300 miles. We are a little older and a little further away. In 2004 Friend agrees 'Image Music Text' is a good name for the gallery: something that follows whatever turns, displaces, shifts, disperses. The name is an egg. This is the first act of the fifth mouth.

IMT may or may not be a generic white cube space. Although sometimes it appears to be (and does so as a necessary part of its blending in with the sector), it has become clear through talking to people we have worked with over the last 17 years[1] how little it resembles this. We create a hybrid through implanting an egg under the skin of an archetype. This is not a generic model for gallery practice, but rather an extraordinary model whose form and function are built through a combination of our desires and our efforts to sustain them.

IMT is also a view from a certain periphery. The candy is held in the corner of the mouth by the tongue. The artworld is not as homogeneous as discourse would often suggest. Although influence and cultural capital clearly seem to coalesce within specific areas, IMT's connectivity to the idea of a homogeneous artworld

DOI: 10.4324/9781003197959-11

is imagined. Its connectivity is to a series of art worlds, dependant on different types of thread: academic affiliations; visibilities in media (art magazines and online blogs); friendships with artists, writers, curators, gallerists and other artworkers and, of course, collectors.

Being a peripheral object connected to a series of worlds, rather than a component of a homogenized whole does not make IMT necessarily outside of that whole. It is easy to forget the route people take to reach small galleries, and through which these spaces are therefore seen. For the most part the visiting of art is through channels of lower resistance, such as the major, publicly funded institutions of towns and cities. As such even the small galleries are viewed as nodes of an ecosystem that connects to the larger national institutions. The UK has, historically, a particularly class-based relationship to these kinds of institutions that is relevant here. The early 19th century impressed upon the working class the value of visiting art collections for instilling patriotic fervour and celebrating the colonial power of the Empire, partly to pre-emptively avoid civil unrest. Here Britain's narrative of power became explicitly defined by its representations of its own cultural activity as well as its representations of Otherness. The nature of Western art history (and from this, much of the cultural signifiers and structures that define contemporary gallery culture) unfolds from an orthodoxy of values that is explicitly colonial. Even the increasing representation of marginalized subjectivities is often, consciously or unconsciously, co-opted into a narrative of British exceptionalism (the exceptionalism of taming dissenting voices) and the moderating of cultural activities (Ziherl 2016, Murphy 2010) within contemporary gallery practices can still be read as a means to reinforce the accuracy of the canon. As such IMT is at a periphery but also at the centre of creative activity in terms of being tied to the traditions of a very particular kind of representation of such activities.

Note

1 2005–22 at time of writing.

11 The Dream at the Periphery of the Centre

IMT, a double imposter, contemplates its own absence. We wish somehow to silence the first mouth and fulfil a desire to encounter the process of writing and reading from outside. In the third mouth the candy dissolves slowly, contaminating then overwhelming with its flavour. The taste of the Visitor slips away, a residue of exotic saliva becomes a memory. The candy, a shape formed in the architectures of both of our mouths, becomes a sliver: a chip on the tongue. Ambiguous, then generic and then gone.

I have described a hybridity that fluctuates between desire for autonomy and community. As Valentine describes in their reading of Hardt and Negri's *Empire* (2004), these tendencies (the effects of organizational heterogeneity, for example) are visible throughout contemporary power structures, of which an art gallery is one. The art gallery is a power structure that reflects, and contributes to, the cohesion of the power structures of contemporary capitalism. IMT, as an art gallery – a mediator of cultural activity, is tied to problematic traditions of representation of such activities. Our attempts at recognizing and short-circuiting some of this harm have impacted on the IMT's various turns, displacements, shifts, and dispersals that enable IMT's unsettledness. I don't argue for their success, only to identify how they played out and what we might learn from this playing out. IMT's history, building towards the space becoming explicitly a gallery proposition, adds some implications and resonances to think back to later: a gallery project as a communal or group responsibility, the attitudes and aesthetics of an artist studio, and the perceived value of proximities

DOI: 10.4324/9781003197959-12

and placing of oneself (both physically and organizationally) within an existing diagram of these proximities.

Bethnal Green, where you can find IMT, is on a canal of warehouse buildings turned into flats. Bourdieu would condemn this site. When we started IMT we felt we were occupiers of spaces and practices that were the domain of business, that we were hackers of enterprise. The archetypal origin story of the art gallery is the existence of affluent connections, financial reserves, or access to credit and parental support (see, for example, Winkleman 2009:8).[1] Friend had none of these but had already formed a collective of people[2] looking to start a small art studio for fabrication and photoshoots, and that could occasionally be made public. A key concern was identifying a place in London within reach of connections she had built whilst studying Fine Art at London Metropolitan University. Without access to significant capital, Friend's financial access to the means of obtaining a space for an art gallery at that time was through two factors: having a group of like-minded allies to share the financial burden of starting and running a space and finding affordable live/work rental property that was available without significant upfront costs. The latter is evidently a significantly more challenging proposition, with other implications following the financial crash of 2008.

Not set up as a formal organization, the space Friend found was given the name Space TwoTenTwo, after its address 210, unit 2,[3] a common naming system shared by galleries in both the commercial and non-profit sectors and a nominative indifference which lends flexibility and speculation to any coming practice or utility. The spelling out of TwoTenTwo (as opposed to 210-2) appears to make this openness intentional. It says to outsiders: we don't know exactly what it is that we are, but we are confident in this unknowing. The first thing TwoTenTwo became was a studio/exhibition space for the collective at the front with Friend living in rooms at the rear of the gallery. Halfway between the V&A Museum of Childhood and the adult entertainment venue Metropolis in Bethnal Green, it was near to some established galleries including the Whitechapel Gallery to the south, SPACE HQ to the north on Mare Street, Maureen Paley and the Wilkinson. The area was felt to be growing in its cultural significance due, in part, to the availability of affordable studios, and would lead to the rise and fall of the nearby Vyner Street as a gallery hotspot. Despite struggling to generate funding, TwoTenTwo would manage to function like this from 2003 to 2005, with members of the studio group sharing the financial responsibility of renting the space.

By 2004 all the members of the group, except for Friend and Wilks, had departed to pursue other activities or had plans to leave. To work on keeping the space functioning as an art gallery Friend was looking to expand the group. I joined TwoTenTwo in 2004 whilst they were in the final stages of planning an exhibition by John Walter and Mark Epstein.[4] By this point, without continuous studio occupancy, it had become a space dedicated far more to exhibitions than studio space or photoshoots, and Friend was keen to see how it could be formalized in some way as a gallery, beyond the loose remit of an artist-run space.

Following a December exhibition of sight-unseen purchasable artworks,[5] TwoTenTwo began work on its penultimate exhibition: a new major installation of an updating of 1992 multimedia work *Kiner* by Polish video artist Józef Robakowski. This show, titled *A View from Elsewhere* (2005), had been organized by curator Pawel Kaminski and the international reputation of Robakowski changed not only our ambitions for the space but also brought attention from other places. Following meetings with McNeill prior to her departure from the gallery, the Wilkinson had proposed that they should, as an established commercial gallery, host the new *Kiner* work, known as *Kiner II* or *Telekiner*, whilst TwoTenTwo should host a group exhibition of animation work by Robakowski's students from the PWSFTViT in Łódź. Standing up to the assumptions of authority of a more established, commercial gallery McNeill had refused. She felt Space TwoTenTwo had committed the effort to organize the project and should be the hosts of the more significant work. This was a deal breaker for the Wilkinson. Both took place subsequently at TwoTenTwo.

Kiner was a fragile, kinetic installation that acted as an evocative and stark metaphor for the recent history of media in moving image art in Poland. In Poland in the 1980s, the Polish People's Republic attempted to suppress political opposition by introduction of martial law. This move had a major impact on Polish experimental film by restricting artists' access to the equipment and facilities they needed. In its place artists turned to video. Although this was a shift that had already taken place to some degree as artists sought to bypass film facilities to more immediately access the means of production,[6] it forced a broader range of artists to embrace video technology as their medium.[7] *Kiner* consisted of a line drawn into film, rotating around the height and length of the gallery, the tape clicking and slipping slightly as it loops. It must be regularly repaired, sections occasionally cut out and reconnected with tape. The film is recorded by a video camera as it moves, digitized, and then projected onto the wall with a digital projector: a continuous projected, hand drawn line running up the wall of the gallery.[8] These three stages, film to video to digital, represented, for Robakowski (1977), an allegory that provides a technohistorical and geopolitical context (the chronological movement from film, to video to digital) for his ongoing interests in the translation of acts of his 'psychophysical organism' through mechanical recording devices.

At this point some of the details become cloudy. Robakowski's work sold to Tate, but via other agencies. TwoTenTwo did not receive any commission for the sale, a lesson that would have implications for some later decisions about gallery commission. Yet the show brought unexpected interest and we start to appear on mailing lists for more exclusive events, including private exhibitions designed to promote new works by established artists.

The success of the Robakowski exhibition as a show of, what we believed to be, important, insightful, and accessible contemporary work that we'd helped to make happen, and its perceived success outside of our social circle (within some vague concept of establishment art world) cemented a decisive factor in TwoTenTwo's legacy with respect to IMT. *Kiner* was a fragile, kinetic installation and so resisted commodification, and Polish migration to the UK in 2004, the year that Poland joined the EU, was the subject of paranoid and xenophobic tabloid and right-wing media narratives around infrastructure, property prices, jobs, an imagined predisposition to criminality, and the fear of money been sent out of the country. As such, *A View from Elsewhere*, showing that Poland could also be the source of critically compelling contemporary art by both established and young artists, a reality that should have been self-evident, was nonetheless significant. The making-visible of art makers of different levels of visibility, and the public interchange of their work, would become a founding concern for IMT.

A View from Elsewhere began two relationships integral to the early direction of IMT: the curator Pawel Kaminski, who would go on to curate an annual project with the gallery up until 2012,[9] and the Polish Cultural Institute, which would provide small but significant project funding for exhibitions with Polish artists. However, with McNeill having left TwoTenTwo to pursue an MA, and with me having joined, TwoTenTwo was ending in a very different composition from how it had begun, and Friend was keen to formalize our activities into a new project that could somehow sustain itself. This also became an opportunity to address the openness of TwoTenTwo and propose a series of ethical and curatorial propositions.

Notes

1 Winkleman gives the example of Jen Bekman raising start-up costs by cashing in her government pension, 'maxing out her credit cards' and sleeping on the floor of her mother's apartment as a viable alternative, an example that only replaces one form of privilege with another (8).

2 Julian Latorre, Aidan McNeill, Daniel Whibley, and Gemma Wilks.

3 The gallery is made up of two large main rooms, a kitchen, and bathroom, with high ceilings and large windows facing Cambridge Heath Road at the front and a car park and residential entrances at the rear. It has a spiral staircase leading to an upper mezzanine level, which is also part of the property. It is in Bethnal Green, East London, on Cambridge Heath Road between Parmiter Street and Patriot Square. Its location is close to Cambridge Heath Road station (WAGN Railways), and both Bethnal Green Underground (on the Central line) and Bethnal Green (WAGN Railways) are also nearby.

4 *Delayed Gratification* (2005).

5 *Shop* (2004).

6 As well as allowing artists to circumvent technicians (who were for the most part white men) facilitating more moving image works by and of marginalized, countercultural, or hidden groups.

7 See also for a more global context the revolutionary potential of the Sony Portapak DV-2400 Video Rover in 1967, the same year that Marshall McLuhan and graphic designer Quentin Fiore produced the influential *The Medium Is the Message: An Inventory of Effects*, subsequently released that same year as a vinyl LP:

> Societies have always been shaped more by the nature of the media by which [we] communicate than by the content of the communication [...] The living room has become the voting booth. Participation

via television in Freedom marches, in war, revolution, pollution, and other events is changing everything.

(McLuhan and Fiore 1967:22)

8 The 1992 version of the work was yet to include the digitization process.
9 Laura Pawela's *Sweet Heart Now Grown So Cold* (2012).

12 Collectivity and 'a Plan of Living'

Although the architectural space was to remain the same, we wanted this new project to be built as a conceptual project as much as a practical one, but which would seek to address some of the practical lessons learnt during TwoTenTwo's run. These lessons involved the failure to attract funding; the lack of formal business structure (which made applying for funding restrictive); and the aim to reach an audience beyond TwoTenTwo's immediate circle of friends and collaborators. Friend was also keen to break with TwoTenTwo's practice of space rental (IMT would not offer the gallery for hire for public exhibition). Whilst gallery hire is a potential business, we felt that public rental might undermine the sense of this new project as a project with an identity and praxis.[1]

We made a series of declarations. The first was that the gallery was a work, or practice, that would replace our own artwork during the time we'd devote to it and that our own artwork wouldn't be exhibited in the gallery other than through our practice as gallerists. For Friend this was about changing the mode of her practice from the making of objects to investigating their existence in a wider context: 'My practice as an artist was shifting into making exhibitions, and *artist-as-business*. I'm not sure what "serious" meant for me back then, but it was about this shift to being taken seriously' (Friend 2022, personal communication, 28 December). Karl England, artist and co-founder of the mutable arts organization Sluice, understands this as visible in some, but not all, gallery projects led by artists seeking to align the art with the mode of representation:

DOI: 10.4324/9781003197959-13

Organisation / Infrastructure / Platform _as_ creative endeavour as opposed to mere scaffolding for creative endeavour is a position the artist-led project alone can occupy. [The] artist-led project [allows for] an authenticity [to] exist between artistic intent, delivery and display that commercial and institutional platforms cannot manufacture.

(England 2022, personal communication, 29 January)

This emphasis, not art-as-business but artist-as-business, supports a conceptualization of spaces like IMT in relation to Foucault's 'arts of existence' (1984) and Deleuze's 'invention of a people' (1985:217): i.e. that IMT as *artist*-as-business is at first, for Friend, their invention of themself, but then also, as a part of this, an orientation of IMT towards their invention of a people (an audience and a community).

The second decision we made was ethical: first IMT was to be instituted as a non-profit company limited by guarantee, legally directing potential profits to supporting the gallery's activities, and second stipulating that if there was money available, it would go first to artists showing at the gallery. Only if the artists had been paid would we be paid. We were unemployed, with no savings, looking for work that would fit around running the gallery, but we knew our position (as gallerists in command of an affordable space) had benefits. We were aware from our experience as artists that usefully running a gallery will rely on the contributions of artists (in terms of their time, labour, artwork), and that these benefits we hold in renting and managing the space could be exploited to help artists rather than be used as a means of providing our own income. How, given our financial situations, were we able to do this? As Sansone Ruiz explains, speaking to me over Zoom in 2021:

Karl England came up with [a theory that] everyone has an art world secret. Either you have property, that you don't pay money on; you're independently wealthy, someone supports you; or you're not actually making it at all. And I feel like the art world secret of IMT is that you guys lived in the gallery. Your living room was the gallery office, and your bedroom was upstairs. It's a small but significant detail. It's become very fashionable now in New York in the last few years to push the furniture aside and have apartment galleries. But you lived in the gallery, like in a crawl space, you wouldn't have even known that there was a bedroom upstairs. You're like a giant man who lived in a small space. And you guys were able to cater events because that was your kitchen. Birthday parties happened in the gallery.

(Sansone Ruiz 2021, personal communication, 12 October)

This approach allowed for significantly lower rent and overheads in an increasingly more expensive area. It is our secret.

However, there are other consequences to this mode of living. As Sansone Ruiz makes clear, this is not a gallery in a home, this is a gallery/home hybrid,[2] nothing is pushed aside. The material environment is an inescapable and ever-present reminder of hybrid conditions. The building guides the unsettlement of activities that take place or are imagined here, always reorienting through bodies and affordances.

There is, in this mode, a danger of turning everything, every social interaction, into content or practice. In the gallery, in IMT, art operates in the same space as a toilet. A kitchen (we have mouths to feed). An office table is a dining table. Places for bodies and the things that come out of them and go into them to keep them from falling apart. There are so many more interactions at IMT than the enunciation of relations to discourse and the accumulation of capital.

Coming out of Fine Art degrees, we were accustomed to hybridizing life and work,[3] and of a working together of theory and practice. Our ideas for IMT developed around ideas of what we thought art should be rather than what we could do to make a successful business out of the management of creative practices. There is a tendency to look back on this considering contemporary curatorial theorizing or in terms of theories of business management in the cultural industries. In the case of IMT however it is precisely our lack of engagement with such a theorized context that gives rise to the project's hybridized organizational experimentalism.

Galleries, as much as or perhaps more so than other forms of social space, attempt to assume an outward face of neutrality (Lefebvre 1991:249). This neutrality is only readable as such for those who have already bought into the idea of an art world as a homogenized means to represent human creative diversity. For others, no matter how much art institutions might attempt to open themselves up to a community, the diversity of the communities that organizations place themselves within are rarely represented within the gallery (whether through artist, worker, or audience). Part of this is due to the separation of the gallery's architecture from the spaces of the street.

Maleuvre summarizes the key function of the museum in how it defines our encounters as a question of authenticity. He claims that the museum removes things from their original locations and into a place where they are no longer lived with other than as things to be 'gawked at' by the visitor (1999). Like the University in Harney and Moten's *The Undercommons* (2013), the museum, and by extension the art world, is stolen life. We can relate this directly to the contemporary art gallery also, and to the images of cultural history they build, albeit shortening the space between origin and display.

Burrows describes IMT's differential as a disinterest in the museum's function:

> Nobody I work with has got an eye on [history or] being in the Tate collection or in a Thames and Hudson book. I think it's all about the present. Most things [we make] do get thrown away. Plastique Fantastique are part of a scene and there are fellow travellers. And IMT is a scene, which people look to. So, I think that's where things get their value. When things go into a museum it's just sort of weird ... like necrophilia.
>
> (Burrows 2021, personal communication, 26 October)

But there is another orientation: mind–body dualism. George A. Romero shows this is a myth, even the modern zombie, the ultimate mindless body, has vestiges of self. But galleries often seek to identify with 'Mind, modernism's greatest invention' (O'Doherty 1999:87), to separate art into an illusion of pure contemplation. This is why so many galleries make it difficult to be a body. Both separate, one from life the other from body. IMT occupies a more unsettled differential between living space and exhibition space: Sphynx cats prowl amongst the art, leaping at phantom birds in video projections; a gallery with a kitchen used to cook breakfast; an artist-as-business; an artwork is a door handle;[4] an organization interested in grooving with others; a body rejecting its separation. Ruskin might reject the Penanggalan as a multiplication of the feeding of the stomach rather than the mind. But there is no threshold here, the stomach has a mind that speaks through the guts and can play a flute with its ass.[5]

According to Fernández, the digital has created a problem which infers that, from summarizing Deleuze, Guattari, Massumi, and Grosz, 'works of art should no longer be conceived as static autonomous entities but as *evolving processes* that unfold in relation to both user and environment' (Fernández in Donald Preziosi 2009:468, original emphasis). Given these realities, how can this separation of body and mind maintain itself in our white cube galleries and defend its removal of objects from the world?[6] Close the first mouth again.

In 2005 my own understanding of critical theory was relatively patchy, aside from Burroughs, I had read Solanas and Artaud, especially the Theatre of Cruelty manifestos. Old texts for a young discipline. Artaud's 'No More Masterpieces' and Solanas' discussion of 'great art' from the *SCUM Manifesto* appear to be so antithetical to the idea of a curatorial that they almost are anti-curatorial.[7] Artaud rejects the masterpiece, but he is also familiar with the first mouth: the mouth through which the masterpiece is announced. He rejects the masterpiece's disconnection from life ('art on the one hand and life on the other') and its irrelevance as a vestige of the past ('once spoken, all speech is dead and is only active as it is spoken' 56). Artaud is seeking a theatre relevant to 'the masses' and to life as lived, rather than a theatre only real within the constructed value systems of an elite. His demand is that things happen, are lived; and that this lived art, with its inherent danger, is where art is most valuable (and has its widest audience). Artaud wants the first mouth to close and the other mouths to devour it. Solanas has a not dissimilar take. She maintains that what she derisively calls 'Great Art' is made to solve the 'dilemma of not being able to live [...] by constructing a highly artificial world'. As with Artaud, Solanas calls for a recognition of this work's falseness, its separation from lived experience. I read SCUM as a narrative describing hegemony, Solanas describes the holding of cultural authority over those supressed and marginalized. For Solanas, under patriarchy, the artist as society knows them is sought for insights by the inadequate and confused authority, whereas in Solanas' utopia, 'the only Art, the only Culture, will be conceited, kooky, funky, females grooving on each other and on everything else in the universe' (1971:60).

For Solanas, art-making is accessible on the basis of enjoying each other and the universe rather than a unrealistic (in being unreal) demonstration of cultural authority in accordance with the power structures that sustain this authority. There can be no dead museums in Solanas' utopia.

From this interest in art being inextricable from life, politics and present time, and the utopian vision of engaging with the universe (and each other), I had in these early days read Timothy S. Murphy's *Wising up the Marks* (1997) that positioned Burroughs in relation to both Bruno Latour's *We Have Never Been Modern* (1991) and Ralph Ellison's *Invisible Man* (1952) and what I got from it (and from then reading Latour, but also, more effectively, from reading Ellison) was this emphasis on 'a plan of living'. Murphy defines Ellison's text as describing a 'plan of living' that aims to articulate:

> collectivities that defy representation, these new Harlems occupying the edges of our social perceptions and the gaps between our political categories, in both senses of the word *articulate*: analyse them, criticize them, *speak* them within the space of language; but also extend, enact, and *construct* them within the social and material spaces that are irreducible to that space.
>
> (Murphy 1997:33)

For Murphy this is a project that unfolds also through Deleuze (through the multiplicity) and Burroughs (through the disruption of the state language, such as 'family talk, mother talk, father talk, cop talk, priest talk, country talk or party talk' [1969] that, as in Foucault, regulate life). For Burroughs language is used to control, stigmatize, and remove those who do not respond favourably to the frames created by such systems. The first mouth as gatekeeper.

Burroughs' interest in actively engineering autonomy from causality, his experimentalism, and his search for different, creative systems of evading a central power, is difficult not to tie to his biography. There are things that it is easy to be sympathetic with: the impact his addictions and the social views on homosexuality contemporary to him undoubtedly had on his life and those around him, his distrust of law enforcement and imagining of anarchist communities. Yet these do not in themselves appear to herald the extremes of his practice. It is problematic to overlook the role other biographical influences may have had in this work: his neglect of his children; his contribution to his wife's misery and eventual death by his hand; his thirst for binaries, misogyny, and distaste for effeminate men; his apparent support of paedophilia, and his stance on a kind of individualist libertarianism that included his adamant anti-abortion beliefs and pro-gun rhetoric, positions that seem at odds with the counterculture of his time. Burroughs is not a romantic figure and anyone finding him so would do well to check out Rob Johnson's *The Lost Years of William S. Burroughs: Beats in South Texas* (2006) for an extended account of his abuse and killing of Joan Vollmer as well as *Cursed from Birth: The Short, Unhappy Life of William S. Burroughs, Jr.* (2006), his son's autobiographic account of his own final years before his early, alcohol-induced death. It is also clear that Burroughs' neglect for those who depended on him emotionally and for care is strikingly visceral. James Grauerholz's account of their relationship in the 'Death of Joan Vollmer Burroughs', Ted Morgan's biography and *The Lost Years* all give accounts of this – and his 'disingenuous' connection of her killing to his literary career (Grauerholz 2002:60–1) especially understanding this connection as a confession that Joan had become a hindrance to his freedom and career rather than (as it is mostly interpreted in his favour) as some kind of magical writer spell. Even those with which we might have less sympathy: the Church of Scientology, for example, recounted with frustration, through my interview with David Gaiman, how Burroughs had difficulty treating with courtesy those who supported him (Gaiman 2008, personal correspondence, 9 April). As such, Burroughs' project is poisoned by some clearly terrible behaviours and apparent beliefs, and rather than being solely an altruistic exercise to free humanity of control, can be read as a far more venal freedom from the effects of his own actions. It should be clear that IMT, and indeed many others who've deployed Burroughs' various methods, not least D&G, Kathy Acker, as well as feminist literary criticism of the early 1990s, do so for their emancipatory potential for groups of people rather than that of individual authors.

For IMT as a 'Plan of Living', a project entangled with our living bodies, this is what we tried to do. We extracted from our social surroundings ideas that we thought could contribute to such a plan of living from our own limited, and different, perspectives. Art's value seemed to fall between a set of trajectories: the romantic ideal of freedom of expression, a means of articulating identity and/or humanity, a place for debate, a vehicle for social commentary, the market commodified, perhaps a social good in-and-of-itself through granting agency to those otherwise without.

As a gallery, we were to look at how a gallery might function to combine social and work functions without each erasing the other. We would use language primarily as a disruptor, and a means of challenging how artists are described and compartmentalized.

The gallery as a tool to 'articulate [...] collectivities that defy representation' was admittedly limited to our immediate environment (to the *within reach*) but expanded quickly, and our attempts to 'extend, enact, and *construct* them within the social and material spaces that are irreducible to that space' would have varying degrees of success. Yet the essential theme was that we believed there were ways in which we could show that contemporary art had value to everyone, even if this meant a collapsing of what contemporary art was supposed to be.

Some infrastructure implications of this had already arrived from other sources. My knowledge of arts infrastructure had come from studying at the Slade, which in 2000–2 generally privileged finding existing avenues of display. So, in my naivety, the mere notion of starting a space from scratch seemed to have the potential to be a radical act. I felt that commercial galleries were not for me as a visitor, nor as an artist. I'd performed as part of an art band at a Bruce McLean performance *Rubbish Dump Developments and Anti-Social Housing: An Animated Speech* at Anthony d'Offay Gallery in 2001, but the band had then been ruthlessly steered away from the post-event drinks.[8] I was more comfortable, and regular, at performances in studios, or in bars like the Foundry, Old Street, a dishevelled but lively bar with a basement which hosted unpredictable art events.[9] It is no accident that the quiet of the gallery favours the first mouth, whilst the cacophony of a bar is far more suited to the others.

Friend had a more applied experience of gallery function and social practice, having been working for Richard Hylton at Unit 2 Gallery, whilst Hylton was working on research that would lead to his book *The Nature of the Beast: Cultural Diversity and the Visual Arts Sector* (2007) an analysis of the impact of cultural diversity policies and initiatives on Black artists. She also had access to the critical stance of her tutors Nico de Oliveira and Nicola Oxley who were running the Museum of Installation (1990–2005) with Michael Petry, a non-profit space that devoted itself entirely to installation, avoided sales and funded itself via project grants. As such Friend was more in tune with grassroots infrastructure in London, the ecological nature of its existence and the real ends to which it could be put, whereas my concerns came more from so-called radical philosophy, interest in esoteric, punk, industrial and experimental culture and a less located (i.e. more general) understanding of its potential value.

Feeling unattached from and unsupported by what we understood to be the art world we built our plan of living, based around the effort to articulate those collectivities that we understood were defying representation, and to seek out the gaps between (political) categories as we understood them. Some of this work had already, in retrospect, appeared at TwoTenTwo through a series of solo exhibitions by queer artists, and the Robakowski exhibitions that countered contemporary public perception.

It was only with our new critical focus however that we began to discuss this as a strategy, a plan of living, and to proceed then to *articulate* (re: Murphy 1997:33) these collectivities through practice in social and material terms. Although the size of the space meant that exhibitions were most often by solo artists, nonetheless, the idea of collectivities remained a focus in terms of how artists were connected to collectivities, or indeed were part of collaborations or collectives as their art practice. These considerations have a considerable effect on how a gallery understands its audience as well as the network of artists and cultural workers with which it is connected, however it was a particular focus on collectivities, rather than spectacle, with which we were concerned and this was ideologically counter to trends of the 1990s that had become a familiar framing of successful artistic activity.

Notes

1 We still occasionally offered the gallery for private rental: including acting classes, meetings and porn shoots.
2 There is also an ethical benefit to a home within a closed gallery. The inhabitants (currently Lindsay and three cats) would otherwise need

affordable space elsewhere. The cats help. When Lindsay goes away, she offers her living space to others in exchange for feeding the cats.

3 This particular hybridizing of life and work does not extend to its post-social media practice, of which more later.

4 Gordon Shrigley in *Attachment* (2013) – after reading the first draft of this book, Friend persuaded Shrigley to reinstate this work as a permanent feature in the space.

5 Such playing is, according to Harris' analysis of *Naked Lunch*, indicative of extraordinary, uninhibited improvisation. See Harris 2003:237.

6 In their analysis of Shu Lea Cheang's porno booths in *Those Fluttering Objects of Desire* (1992) Jury et al. suggest the idea that 'the body *is* the informational infrastructure'. They maintain that Cartesian mind/body dualism is 'central to the types of subjectivities imagined and reproduced by digital virtuality' and that Cheang's work instead places 'the corpus [as] the primary sources of perception, knowledge and connection' (Jury et al. 2018: 15).

7 Russell's *Glitch Feminism* updates these demands to a communal, technologically aware, racially aware form. But see also 'DEMOLISH ART MUSEUMS' 'DEMOLISH SERIOUS CULTURE' by Jack Smith and Tony Conrad, protesting outside MoMA, NYC, 27 February 1963.

8 McLean, who was teaching at the Slade at the time, had asked us to play, punctuating his performance, after we had played him the recording of a previous gig. The band *Eabarotrauma* was essentially a chaotic noise improvisation outfit. As I remember it, we became disillusioned by the power dynamics and feeling we were being instrumentalized by both the gallery but also by some new artists who'd joined the band only for this specific event, and we disbanded shortly afterwards.

9 It is gone now. Currently, at the time of writing, its former home is under development as 'an arts and premium lifestyle hotel': www.pphe.com/brands/artotel Accessed 11 August 2022.

13 The Long 1990s

Technique Anglaise: Current Trends in British Art (1991) edited by Andrew Renton and Liam Gillick, with Lynne Cooke, William Furlong, Maureen Paley, and Karsten Schubert, gives some indication of the scepticism of the moment. The authors suggest artists have 'out-minimalised each other and out-conceptualised each other, so where now? [...] Why be alternative when the alternative has already become mainstream?' (40). And yet: 'there's no shared idealism going on' (39) these are individuals 'playing for time' (40). There is in *Technique Anglaise* a sense of boredom, defeat, individualism, the shadow of neoliberalism. It focuses on an impasse. A sense of lack. The lack of the New. A symptom perhaps of Mark Fisher's slow cancellation of the future. A series of images of crowds at exhibitions, presented in black and white, is an illustration of the lifeblood of an art scene, drained.[1]

In 1998 the artist David Burrows organized the conference *Who's Afraid of Red, White and Blue* at the University of Central England, Birmingham, where Michael Corris described how he thought the society of spectacles was at the centre of what artists were doing. According to Burrows:

> [Corris] thought that in the '90s what happened was that a group of artists understood that visibility was capital, and that instead of working together to build institutions and communities they just wanted to be visible within the media, and if you're visible within the media, if [...] TV presenters like you and get you into magazines, collectors are gonna buy you.
>
> (Burrows 2021, personal communication, 26 October)

DOI: 10.4324/9781003197959-14

This was the framing of art practice, specifically Young British Art practice, that we'd been exposed to as art students as the dominant mode. The first mouth is faulty and its articulations are techniques of power only. Licking Einstein's brain sliver gives no access to his thought, only an initiation hazing into a hegemonic fraternity.

There were of course organizations that explicitly resisted the focus on the autonomous individual even as it was becoming the model of professional practice in art schools. In 1996 artists Ruth Catlow and Marc Garrett started Furtherfield, a community and collaboration-focused organization that attempted exactly that, a positioning against what they saw as the exclusive nature of the commercial art world, but also challenging some of the infrastructures of state on which the academy is also dependant. Despite Furtherfield's resolute positioning against art world infra-structure, rather than co-opting commercial activity as a survival strategy,[2] they have achieved a long-term stability. Their work, from the positioning of the outside, depending upon an art-istic community and the philosophies and tools that grew out of activism, community art, pirate radio and the free and open soft-ware cultures to deconstruct and de-territorialize arts practices (See Catlow and Rafferty 2022 and Catlow et al. 2017).

Valuable activist-affiliated organizations such as Furtherfield were often less visible to many young artists moving thorough mainstream institutions. So, it was the work of artists collectives like Bank, of which Burrows was briefly a part in the early 1990s, that were presented as antagonistic alternatives and dir-ectly affected IMT's starting conditions, explicitly using art world systems against themselves, especially in its use of language in parodic exhibitions and texts. Burrows has seen these approaches to have become more central to the desires of art makers, identi-fying the role of community and collectivity as means by which to counter the prevailing ethos of the 1990s.

Although we lacked the imagination and audacity to set our-selves up outside of art world dynamics, IMT was nonetheless named IMT as a collectivity. Friend wanted to resist the indi-vidualistic connotations of the Lindsay Friend Gallery, or even the kinds of riffs on this taken by galleries like Matt's Gallery[3] or the ill-fated Keith Talent Gallery (named after a fictional char-acter in the Martin Amis novel *London Fields* [1999]).[4] The name IMT was a cypher, something we could project onto, yet could also outgrow its material conditions without the located emphasis of TwoTenTwo.

The building of a 'plan of living': articulating collectivities through collective responsibility, an artist studio ethos, and the creative negotiation of existing structures give the outline of this hybrid. However, there are also key considerations here as to how the organization of the gallery came into being. IMT's appearance relied on conditions that may have been scarce in 2005 yet are now significantly scarcer. In the case of Friend, it is collaboration and community that enabled IMT to exist in the first place, and even now, whilst the resources to start a space like IMT are scarcer and likely to be, in many cases, outmoded, collaboration and community is likely to remain the most ethical and workable solution. Yet, having access to a building in London to repurpose was ultimately what made it a gallery, and it is the lack of such resources that have become seriously inhibitive for new projects at the time of writing.

This is not to denigrate IMT's success at survival. For Pawel Kaminski, coming to IMT from outside the UK, IMT surviving its location was a marker of success, alongside two other markers: the focus on sound art from 2005 to 2010 and the formation of a group of people:

> IMT [succeeded by] simply surviving in Zone 2 of London Underground. Many did not. Also we all succeeded (as far as I know) by creating long lasting friendships.
> (Kaminski 2021, personal communication, 4 October)

Yet already, in the early part of the 2000, the possibilities of being in an accessible location like Bethnal Green, were becoming increasingly rare. As Friend recalls: 'There was a shift away from creating live/work units in nearby Hackney as people were taking advantage of the system and essentially using them as residential' at a time that the area was concerned about loss of commercial properties (Friend 2021, personal communication, 3 December). However, it is important to acknowledge that the affordability of space that allowed IMT to appear no longer exists, especially following the financial crash of 2008. As such our claim on visibility is privileged by the time (2003) when Friend discovered this space, as well as accidents that allow it to continue as property rented by IMT.

Notes

1 This book connects to IMT through the people in it: Renton was to teach me at the Slade. Furlong's Audio Arts helped me rethink how the art I was making could be simultaneously an archive or a field recording. He would hear Earbarotrauma play at the Bruce McLean event. I would end up occasionally visiting Paley's gallery for openings, as it was a mere ten minutes' walk from IMT at Three Colts Lane.

2 They have made clear on several occasions that they are not interested in the commercial, their rejection of the late 20th century marketization of art being a key influence on the project. See, for example, Catlow and Garrett 2021.

3 The double joke of Matt's Gallery named, in 1979, not after the gallerist (the artist Robin Klassnik), but after his dog, Matt E. Mulsion was a key motivator for IMT's early foundation and, incidentally, has often artists in common in our combined exhibition histories. Yesterday I put on a coat I haven't worn for a while. Whenever I do this the pockets invariably contain a crumpled information sheet from a gallery visit. This one is from Matt's Gallery. The Luke McCreadie exhibition *A length of spit dangled from a mouth* (2019). We had shown McCreadie's work in *Ref...* (2015) after seeing his work first at Grand Union in *Magic Eye* (2013) and then working with him at Gallery North for *The miserable bureaucrats...* (2014). McCreadie might, I think, be the only case where an artist has exhibited at Matt's after IMT rather than the other way round, not counting John Walter's solo exhibition *Booze Guitar* (2018) following *Delayed Gratification* at TwoTenTwo in 2015. But common artists have included: Benedict Drew, Emma Hart, Joey Holder, Melanie Jackson, Tai Shani, and Matt Stokes.

4 London Fields also being the name of a park in Hackney near where the gallery was located, Keith Talent Gallery was supported by studio lets and which also produced the magazine *Miser & Now*. Named after a criminal from the book, in 2009, in a bizarre case of nominative determinism, the co-directors were found guilty of theft and fraud, and one of the directors of forgery, after drawings by Tom of Finland belonging to the permanent collection of the Tom of Finland Foundation were illicitly sold by the gallery to a private collector under forged certificates of authenticity. My abiding memory of Keith Talent was visiting their studio complex and seeing that they were running the electricity for several artist studios from a single overloaded extension cable. The idea that a space that presented itself as a professional organization would put its tenants lives and work at risk taught us to keep our eyes open elsewhere.

14 2008

Space in London, especially as central as Bethnal Green, is finite. The financial crash and the ensuing politics of austerity in the UK have removed what little support there was for artists. Charlotte Warne Thomas' 2021 report 'Artists as Workers' makes it clear that the disappearance or limiting of state benefits that existed for artists prior to 2008 have now reached the state where art-making is once more the preserve of the elite, and thence 'elite artists making art for elite consumption' (2021:40). It was clear after 2008 that the kinds of artist-run, garage spaces that surrounded us were shifting towards temporary galleries run by the children of oligarchs. If galleries became successful, they moved to Fitzrovia, Hoxton or out west; unsuccessful and they were priced out and became peripatetic projects or disappeared entirely.

We have a responsibility, yet at the same time our claim on this space is fragile. Regular appraisals by the landlords haunt our presence there with the knowledge that we are expendable. Yet we can't ignore that being able to rent this space at the time not only make us a good bet to stay (building up faith in our ability to pay rent on time) but also allowed us the time to build reputation (cultural capital) in a way that is no longer accessible to those who live in London.

IMT is therefore an opportunity that no longer exists or is out of reach. There are no longer affordable, viable gallery spaces available, which calls for debate on how alternatives might be sought, or imagination for alternative platforms outside of institutions and art galleries. Part of Warne Thomas' solution is the importance of

DOI: 10.4324/9781003197959-15

subsidizing space (ibid. 80), potentially making projects like IMT once more feasible.

Alternatively, or in addition to, space subsidy, there should be work done to fight for irrecoverable opportunities by holding organizations to account for lack of representation or lack of support for those not afforded such opportunities, speaking from platforms that are being heard (whether these be the universities in which we teach, the social media platforms on which we argue, or the books in which we write). There is an ethical duty of giving access to space that we were fortunate enough to have access to. Giving opportunities to artists and curators who had not had the opportunity to become established when resources were more available and networks more easily located.

15 Being Public

The Threshold and the Café

A mouth is reading:

> Take a walk down a city street and put down what you have just
> seen on canvas. You have seen a person cut in two by a car, bits
> and pieces of street signs and advertisements, reflections from
> shop windows – a montage of fragments.
>
> (Burroughs 1986a:61)

When writing about the 2010 IMT exhibition *Dead Fingers
Talk: The Tape Experiments of William S. Burroughs*, I observed a
child of three or four interacting with an installation by Aki Onda,
First Thought Best Thought (2010):

> A fugitive of identities crossing back and forth, intercutting
> [themself] with [their] environment, switching between play and
> performance [using] sounds as environmental cues to liberate
> [their] actions, [themself] and [their] environment, physical and
> metaphysical, as a montage of fragments. The perpetuation of
> a coherent narrative is not essential for [the visitor's] investiga-
> tion of the work; in fact it would limit it.
>
> (Jackson 2014b:198–9)

This memory, and how I have tried to contain it in text, echoes
through this attempt to illustrate IMT as curatorial practice. Here,
at this point in the text, it becomes most relevant. Burroughs' cut-
ups and fold-ins are unsettlings of what Latour calls 'the work of
purification' in favour of the hybrid, and IMT's curatorialisms are

DOI: 10.4324/9781003197959-16

often a similar shuffling, guided by the technologies of architecture and labour rather than paper and scissors.

From my perspective, as an artist-turned-curator, the organization of art was going to follow my understanding of its making, making-public and critique as I had experienced it as an artist and visitor more than an art historian. I had come to curating via a particular interest in sound art, and in Burroughs' tape experiments, as well as sound art's co-opting of histories of music and performance, which, such as in the case of Jacque Attali (especially Attali 1977), was inextricable from the presence of audiences and the reordering of audience in relation to artist, architecture, appearance, and artefact, in a way less visible in art history. I was interested in how visitors engaged with the work given the resources they carried with them, rather than curating as a means by which a fixed narrative of the work might be passed cleanly from gallery to visitor.

For Cooke, a similar route from a Fine Art degree foregrounded a concern with mediation, through thinking about the encounter with the work. For Friend, it would be through the space as a hybrid domain of home, social, studio, gallery functions. The 'public' in the making public of an exhibition is not pure but a series of transitions, enclosures, frontiers, and voids. Which public does an exhibition reach when it becomes an enclosure?

Towards the end of 2008 we had closed the gallery for a couple of months to allow the artist Maria von Köhler to build an installation: *Maybe a Herm* (2009). It was an exhibition that was about boundaries between things, a herm being a carved stone post or pillar used as a marker for border or periphery. But instead of being a concrete border, von Köhler's herm was a swollen mass of flesh and horns taking up the gallery and presenting its buttocks to the street. It had to be destroyed at the end of the show as it was too large, too located, to fit through the door. The herm is of course a product of Hermes, the god that is a trickster (see, for example, Kerényi [1943] or Hansen [2001]).

As the exhibition was being constructed, one night in 2009, a group of young men attacked Lindsay and me, beat me to the road outside The George and Dragon,[1] and tried to open my head with a piece of masonry. This location marked the threshold of our part of East London, the point at which police officers ask incredulously why we are here, and the world becomes entangled in our inner lives. A marker of the limits of a body and its contents. It is December 2022 as I edit this. I've lost weight. I can run my fingers over where my ribs re-fused; knotted like an old tree.

The herm was also the marker of a different kind of threshold. The Arts Council England declares a change to the application rules for Grants for the Arts applications, essentially ending the practice of applying for shows that run back-to-back. This amendment by the Arts Council felt teleological: to demonstrate the diversity of its supported activities and their validity within the framework of the economy ontology, i.e. a shift away from projects in desperate need of support and instead towards portfolio projects. This significantly limited IMT's ability to fund exhibitions, and instigated a change in the relationships we were to have with artists. All these shifts were Maria's herm demanding a stance and marking the borders between gallery and audience, gallery and artists, gallery and community.

Hansen suggests Hermes is a paradox in that he marks boundaries whilst being a boundary-crosser (2001:38). However, if you are the marker of the threshold, the map maker, you are also privy to its origins as an invention as well as invested in its preservation. IMT is a messy threshold between private home, independent art gallery, and public space. In my conversations, both as curator and educator who teaches art history, there are exhibitions that come up repeatedly as case studies to describe shifts of attention around the theme of exhibition-making and the making public of art: the Independent Group's *This is Tomorrow* at the Whitechapel (1956), which sought to include visitors as participants in the production of culture, and Harald Szeemann's *Live in Your Head: When Attitudes Become Form*, at the Kunsthalle Bern in Switzerland in 1969, in which the gallery became a studio, the curator a collaborator, and the work freed from the walls of the building. In building a gallery and placing art within it, there is an internalized sense of its place, too late for it to be seen in the streets where it might lie mistaken, unratified and kitsch. Yet, like Hermes, we know that the boundaries we have marked between gallery and street are invented even as we happily traverse them, demanding (or assuming) our safety as we do so. Like guardians of culture, who deal in the eternal, and so are immune to death, even the most insubstantial of thresholds can mark a presence.

So, what does the threshold, the herm of the gallery, actually mark? On the one hand it marks IMT, or rather the architectural structure that is read as IMT, as a place that is separate from the publicness of the street. As an art gallery, it is a place that imagines to represent the activity of a public or publics for a public or publics. It is a place that has been made. In a response to the concepts of place understood by Bourdieu, according to Heally (2014), place-making is an active creation of an identity of a location formed through engagement or an activity not usually associated with the function or functions of that place. IMT is an architecture that has been appropriated or intervened into partly because of its failure as an architecture, its structure is suited neither to a business nor a residence, only to a hybrid of both. However, it carries many of what Bourdieu calls the 'cultural products' that allow it to be clearly read, or inscribed, as an art gallery (1979:471), and it does so partly in attempts to establish itself in imitation of other established art spaces. So, the threshold first and foremost marks a space that maintains an uneasy relationship with its outside. This is how IMT is like a mouth. I remember, from *Downcast Eyes*, that for the Greeks the eye was a transmitter as well as a receiver of light (Jay 1993:30), a site of sharing and reciprocation. The mouth still is this, it both takes in and gives out. It is only a threshold that moulds things to its architecture.

Very early on in IMT's programme, having launched an inaugural exhibition,[2] we needed to address this question of threshold. Whereas *Maybe a Herm* took place amidst a paranoid and aggressive atmosphere, *P&S Recipe Shop* (2006) had a more optimistic approach to bodies and thresholds. Firstly, there was an element of trust: restaurants and cafés were opening with a pay-what-you-want ethos, and conversations around relational aesthetics were common even if the forms of work that prioritized the present experience of living gallery visitors were still awkward for galleries to accommodate.

Among Grodach's claims for public value of art galleries are the capability of constantly changing programmes to grant an ability to attract diverse audiences and engage audiences with other experiences they did not specifically come to experience (a claim the Arts Council England's Let's Create Strategy 2020–30 articulates as 'dynamism'). Grodach claims that these are social spaces that allow such audiences to interact with each other, thereby fostering community interaction, and that these spaces simultaneously put these 'communities on display'. And lastly he claims that such spaces bring money to the local area: in our case the increasingly more saturated hospitality industry that especially benefited from post-preview drinks at nearby pubs (Grodach 2009:483–5). These claims are not insignificant and give an alternate ecosystem of community and interaction that isn't entirely prefigured by the money nexus (although it is evidently not separate from it either). *P&S Recipe Shop* was an exhibition by Yak Beow Seah and Chong Boon Pok. Pok and Seah, the latter who was also a cook at a Benihana restaurant, functionally turned the gallery into a cafe in which they served food, sold kitchenware, and chatted with visitors who were invited to pay as they liked. Friend remembers the project in terms of its ability to generate community in a manner that clearly reflects Grodach's findings:

Friend: I remember coming home to IMT having had a shit day putting up with shit from people. And as I walked [onto] the decking [at the front of IMT] there're all these people on Ikea stools in little groups. […] And I got in there and the place was packed, and I went up to [the artists, and asked them] 'is this a group? Does everyone know each other?' and [they] said, 'no, pretty much no one knows anyone'. And it's like ... for me, it did exactly what that show set out to do for them and for us. Can you imagine twenty people all, like, they went out to sit with each other?

(Friend 2021, personal communication, 17 November)

Friend's memory of this project describes a gathering of strangers as friends, a momentary respite from the relentless struggle of a 'shit day putting up with shit from people'. This is a breach of classifications. Shit turns into food. Strangers become friends. An art gallery becomes a café. A café becomes an art installation. Some visitors searching for one find the other. This project evidently taps into the interest in relational art that had, by 2006, become a familiar concern in academia following Rirkrit Tiravanija cooking food for gallery visitors in *Pad Thai* (1990), at the Paula Allen

Gallery in New York, and the publishing of Nicolas Bourriaud's *Relational Aesthetics* in 1998. Pok describes their emphases on the relational in terms of a 'mindfulness to the everyday' (Pok 2021, personal communication, 24 November). He explains that:

> *P&S Recipe Shop* was a project for sharing many aspects of our everyday life and art practice, including the aesthetic we found in the food-related objects that we collected, the aesthetic found in food serving and dining, and the cultural and social elements found in food. [...] It also gave a deep impression and memory to the visitors who came to the exhibition and until today they still discuss the project with me when I meet them, not to mention the friendships I made through the project. [...] Later works after *P&S Recipe Shop* shuttle between the two categories [of everyday objects and everyday activities] through connecting things and people together. The works often take on the elements of collaboration, interaction and [the] socially engaged.

Art here takes place in the social and in the world. Claire Bishop's important text in this vein comes later in 2012's *Artificial Hells*. Here Bishop describes the activation of audience as a key part of the narrative of modernity. The intention here, as Bishop describes it, is emancipatory, in our case from the alienation of a capital-driven and class-oriented artworld. Bishop's key finding here is how she articulates the tension between art and the social along the course of participatory art in the 20th century: 'either social conscience dominates, or the rights of the individual to question social conscience. Art's relationship to the social is either under-pinned by morality or it is underpinned by freedom' (276). This distinction, identified in Boltanski and Chiapello (1999), is also the argument of transferability between art and management (Ancelin-Bourguigon et al. 2019). What *P&S Recipe Shop* made clear in the functions of the everyday was that both Seah and Pok, and IMT, were attempting to do something slightly different. Instead to hold this tension between art and the social. They succeeded in doing so by reducing the resistance of a series of thresholds, those between the open street, hospitality, gallery, and the private space of the home. Nine years later IMT would become the headquarters, in the form of an exhibition, for the artist and architect Gordon Shrigley's candidature for Hackney South and Shoreditch in the 2015 General Election.[3] An exhibition as political manifesto.

We are users and we are part of our own story, everything mediated, 'as if [we] are the centre of attention of a real or imagined audience' (Abercrombie and Longhurst's *Audiences* 1998:89). Handouts exist but are seen instead as another form of making: press releases are written as creative writing. This is, as Cooke explains, partly to explicitly stage 'the curator's voice alongside the artist so that it becomes a tangible structure, resituating where the encounter happens, and what we can expect from the experience with art' (Cooke 2022, personal communication, 28 September). As such, the real question at the heart of the otherness of the visitor is *who is this for*? We can clarify the art experience, the candy exchange, as *instrument*. And when artists explicitly make instruments rather than objects, such as Marek Chołoniewski's *Dark&LightZone* at IMT (2006),[4] as instrument-making artist Krzysztof Wodiczko says so plainly, 'not everyone will make the same art with it' (Wodiczko in Finkelpearl 2001:341).

Notes

1 A popular gay pub that closed in 2015 due to rent increases in Shoreditch.

2 O Zhang *My Little Girl* (2005).

3 *Campaign* (2015).

4 *Dark&LightZone*, curated by Kaminski, turned the gallery into a sound and light synthesizer that responded to the movements of visitors. Lindsay's abiding memory of this is of a boxer creating a soundscape by sparring with the light sensors.

16 Dead Fingers Talk
A Place that Holds

Try to hold ourselves in the third mouth, that point at which the social (Visitor) and artistic (writer) are still unable to know each other but are able to share a candy. How, in this hybrid of public-domestic, the importance is in trying to put strange things (a candy) within reach. Ahmed describes domestic space as 'an effect of the histories of domestication [...] an appropriation of matter [...] transforming "what is strange" into an instrument' (2006:117). The value in art for IMT accordingly is less about the objects themselves but about the experiences they afford. Critical studies talks a lot about the normalization of extreme things, yet Streiber, the third mouth, talks about the paranormalization of the banal. And he does so alongside some of the deeply personal anxieties that come with it.

We are attempting to hold a tension between artistic and social critiques. It is a holding of Streiber and the Visitor together, moving according to their different patterns, exchanging a candy, sticky with saliva. A trace of the Visitor is found in the flipped colonial fantasy of the alien. They are visited by beings with superior tech, they welcome their visitors only to be used and exploited. Most alien abductees are white. Their guilt internalized into vulnerability. We are held by the Visitor, like a baby. Our anuses attended to, its production gathered and whisked away. The last vestiges of candy inspected for resilience.

On page 75 of Kraus' *Social Practices* she writes only, 'The gallery is a place where things are held' (2018:75). What does she mean? Perhaps the page before, just three words: 'POTENTIALITY OR REST'. A holding at the beginning and end of lives and of

DOI: 10.4324/9781003197959-17

things. Sometimes it feels that art is mourning for objects and (if you like) their auras. As it is held, an old photograph comes away from its backing and is pushed aside. The object held in the hands of a gallerist may have a longer presence, yet this doesn't necessarily give it a longer life. It is stored, its image is shared, it is commodified and sold, reproduced, written about and venerated, but mostly hidden in darkness or as a feature of a background. Yet it is the same stupid thing. Its value is all myth. It stands in for sadness.

Memorials (as in Kraus' context), objects of exchange, objects of debt and promise. Held things. Things waiting to be dissolved into a home or archives or commodity or be born into the present. But elsewhere Kraus talks about holding in terms of it being a happiness. For Kraus happiness is 'a clarity or form in which all these fragments of feeling or thought could be magically held' (95). This comes close perhaps to what IMT really hopes to be. A holding of things that we think, rightly or wrongly, might form clarity around our lives. Which, of course, include the lives themselves. When we started IMT, and in the parts at which the most is sacrificed for its maintenance (principally: money, health, relationships, or time), Friend is looking to a point at which IMT will help make her life as the gallery's director worth it all. Hi Lindsay, I am writing to you here. As the gallery folds itself into private lives and plans of living, as it clumsily holds your desires like an imaginary creature all cobbled together, it may be that the means is all there is. So, when we look at the work we do we can look at it as a holding and thereby find its worth.

O'Sullivan writes of holding patterns, things that keep together at minimum consistency. He writes, with Burrows, that Plastique Fantastique is concerned with 'the gathering, mobilization and holding of what we understand as points of collapse' (Burrows and O'Sullivan 2014:254). What do they hold? For Burrows and O'Sullivan, they are 'production and contingency' and holding a production–contingency (patheme-matheme) assemblage (ibid. 255–8). For Plastique Fantastique, holding *is* practice: a repetition or sustained gesture (ibid. 263). But they are also holding patterns for those involved: the different subjectivities that come together and are held for the duration of a performance or series of works. Unlike with Kraus, this kind of holding is only active, there is no rest in the acts of production–contingency, but both Kraus and

Plastique Fantastique identify, in holding, the potentiality/contingency of the act.

There is a third holding whose threads connect to IMT. In *Local Color*, Trueman Capote's travel journal, he calls Tangier 'a basin that holds you'. At least I'm guessing he does. I've never read Trueman Capote. I know the quote because it precedes the prologue of *The Dream at the End of the World*, which I have read, Michelle Green's vivid account of American writers in post-war Tangier (1991). Its quotation is significant however, Green's book is about the Tangier International Zone of Paul and Jane Bowles that then becomes the Interzone of William Burroughs. Interzone is a city moving from international administration control to reintegration as part of the restoration of Moroccan independence of 1956. The Tangier International Zone is at once a promise of (Euro-American) freedom, a heterotopia of artistic creativity, and a bureaucratic 'Kafkian trap' (Harris 2003:180). Enns describes this Tangier/Interzone, via Burroughs, as a space that allows the 'transfer of bodies through walls [through being] converted into units of information that pass freely though barriers without resistance. [A] most perfect illustration of Tomlinson's notion of the deterritorializing effect of media technologies' (2004:111). I can't help but think that such an image, of a place open to the world, governed by a multiple but held under an aegis of economic determinism (Harris 2003:180), is evocative of the cultural institutions of the UK, especially those that construct their identities not around the local but in deference to the 'glamour' of a colonial globalized art world (Marchart 2020:22).[1]

So IMT holds because it is thinking about the things in its hands, also as a holding pattern to create durations of production–contingency, and also as a victim of the economic system that surrounds it (both in the UK and beyond). I said something about the relation of human beings to data in this through my discussion of *This Is a Not-Me*, and Interzone's movement of bodies through walls is only a possibility if one were to assume, as Meta does and the 'Boards, syndicates and Governments of the Earth' (1964:3) insist, that our bodies and or digital identities are the same thing.[2]

Dead Fingers Talk: The Tape Experiments of William S. Burroughs was an exhibition that exercised this kind of holding into a curatorial practice, or rather that this tripartite interpretation of holding works as an appropriate synthesis of its practice.

Dead Fingers Talk typifies IMT's curatorial strategy as a relational studies strategy, an exhibition-as-polylogue both literally and conceptually a 'postmodern [...] cacophony of voices speaking simultaneously' (Reilly 2018:29–30). It took place from 27 May to 18 July 2010 at IMT,[3] with off-shoots at the Wysing Arts Centre, Cambridgeshire (2010),[4] Payne Shurvell Gallery, London (2010),[5] and Galleri Box, Göteborg (2012).[6]

The project was planned from studying Burroughs' tape recordings held at the British Library, where I found their value in their state of being unsettled. They were art that was not art, hybrid, fugitive objects whose meaning varied in time and space (Jackson 2014b). They meant different things for different people, and different things for different disciplines. This cacophony of meanings is fascinating, especially for the relational and, as Reilly identifies in Aiken's analysis of Kristeva, a 'levelling of hierarchy [via] a kind of contemporary barbarism that would disrupt the monological, colonizing centristic drives of "civilization"' (Reilly 2018:30).

It sought to represent contemporary art as beyond the boundaries set up by other approaches, pursing an unsettled domain, like O'Sullivan's holding pattern that attempts to keep an exhibition together at its minimum consistency. I approached a number of artists, writers, musicians and asked them for a response to an idea: the tape experiments of William S. Burroughs, experiments that themselves attempt to resist categorization (see Jackson 2014b).

The curatorial practice was then an act of placing thematically and materially disparate works from different disciplines of making in relation to one another. This was something I'd experimented with before, but only really managed to pursue at IMT. Why? Because the hybrid lends itself to relational studies, the overload of the hybrid diagramming the relational from pattern recognition (re: McLuhan 1964). The curating of the exhibition was attempted as '*a means of investigation* rather than a collection of objects' (Jackson 2010), a phrase I had latched on to via a response by Barry Miles on a question I had about Burroughs' cut-up technique (Jackson 2014b:132). A curatorial practice as an investigation as I understood it was not about the production of an understanding or a fixing of components into a product or spectacle. It was not about knowing what things are and attempting to communicate this knowledge. But instead, it was about searching for a point at which esoteric free play with meaning, or indeed abject joy free of anxiety, might be negotiated. This, coming from Burroughs, appears to reside purely the domain of Bishop's artistic critique, and is, following 'the social turn', out of vogue. From Quaintance (2021): the decade of the 2010s marked 'a switch in sensibility that took the UK art world from a pseudo aesthetic to an ethical regime'.[7] This approach is part of a clear shift also in what is expected of artists and artworks, from the representation of culture to the post-Marxist engineering of social solutions. Come 2021 and the Turner Prize has taken this position, turning its attention to collectives with clear socially engaged priorities and even clearer solutions.[8] We were, however, as much located in the aesthetic as the ethical. At the time I didn't quite get the significance of Solanas' goal of automation in *SCUM* or I may have latched onto that also and been able to achieve more of a balance with the social.

Despite this apparent collapse into explorations of artistic freedom, I would argue that in fact the artistic critique here is also a social critique. This is partly though the possibilities of art to afford contingency, what Burroughs might have understood as art's magical origin (1986a:60), or as Burrows describes it:

> I think a lot of art that is not just for aesthetic judgement and taste and not necessarily a straightforward critique is diagrammatic. What is diagrammatic? Something that presents intelligible relations and then invites a gesture to make something of those relations. So, it's a gesture that invites a gesture. [...] A diagram works on a level that description or words alone don't ... It's like a device you can manipulate in some way. And a lot of art is like that. Like through figure and ground and through working out relations, represented or between things. The Deleuze diagram is only one kind of diagram, but one of the definitions of a Deleuze diagram is a presentation in which multiplicity emerges. And I guess that's also why art is diagrammatic.
>
> (Burrows 2021, personal communication, 26 October)

But it is also in how this mode of curating might disrupt canon. In *Curatorial Activism*, Reilly presents an ethical defence of the relational studies approach to curating. They critique strategies of resistance to the comparative lack of women and non-white artists in major collections and exhibitions, describing how there is a categorization of difference happening and that this is both unjustified and entirely unrepresentative of the diversity of cultural activity. Reilly's criticism of revisionist approaches is that it still maintains the white, masculinist, Western canon at its centre and doesn't deal with the reasons for neglect. Their criticism of area studies is that it maintains the centre and creates peripheries of otherness around this (otherness as a *supplement* to the centre). Relational studies is evidently Reilly's tactic (*Curatorial Activism* is framed as a manifesto), and here Reilly proposes a contemporary art that is beyond the boundaries set up by the other approaches. For Reilly, following Ella Shohat, this is about the ability to 'present multiplicity in terms of an ongoing [...] polylogue' (2018:30). It is a tactic of disruption and of 'perpetual regeneration' (Shohat in Reilly 2018:30), that Jennie Skerl would read in Burroughs as a kind of perpetual revolution (1984), but it is with Reilly that it moves beyond Burroughs' masculinist[9] strategy of achieving freedom into something more usefully social. However, Burroughs' interest in language (via Cooke's reading of Bihrani, a key matrix that makes the West unable to read otherness outside the logic system of the OGU) as a virus also is useful here. Burroughs' viral thinking is one in which language is postulated as a virus from outer space, but Burroughs doesn't understand the virus. He sees the virus as an enemy and as fascist (or as a trigger for fascism) and seeks to take control of it to free himself from the effects of his own actions. Linda Stupart understands the virus. For Stupart it is an agency of mutation disrupting and exploding the stale histories and cultures of misogynism, white supremacy and colonialism and their self-referential infrastructures: 'Bodies quickly learned the way to survive the virus was to be violable, to be porous, to be *lacking in boundary integrity*' and that this state is easier for the 'already objectified, already abject, already broken, already dead' (Stupart 2016:25).[10] The virus moves and replicates and disrupts its host. For Stupart it thrives in the bodies that represent the well-trodden patriarchal narratives of art history and who then, unable to be porous, explode. These are means of addressing the maintenance of narrative control, a theme that others have called to demolish, Gustav Metzger asks us to stop making art for three years[11] an intended destabilizing of capitalism's commercialization of art. Solanas says it all has to end until we are grooving on each other.

O'Reilly's proposition for curatorial practice made me feel so good about what we'd done and the approaches we'd adopted. Yes, I'd say, I agree! And I could point towards our long history of shows by women and non-binary artists and feel that we were being porous. But I am the product of an intersection of privileges and Stupart is right, I don't really know how to be porous.

I had come to Burroughs through a discomfiture of identity, much of which was around language, social behaviour, societal formalities, and grand narratives. Burroughs; sometimes well, sometimes badly; addresses these structures in quite radical ways. Prior to formalizing IMT I had been working on starting a research project around Burroughs, both for academic and exhibition goals, and had become obsessed with *Junky*. There were two things from *Junky* that I would end up carrying with me as cornerstones of my curatorial practice, and which are therefore relevant here:

1 an idea of the fugitive, drawn partly from how Burroughs describes the fugitive nature of language from *Junky*'s Glossary of Jive talk, and partly from Burroughs' interest in communities of fugitives that make appearances in subsequent works, stemming from his obsession with the autobiographic crime novel *You Can't Win* (Black 1926)
2 an idea of an alternative, diagrammatic, map of a particular place – a map whose locations are guided by needs of addicts rather than the intentions of city planners. As O'Sullivan summarizes Deleuze's take on the paintings of Frances Bacon: 'a whole asignifying economy – that disrupts a given signifying order (in this case figuration), allowing a "new" world to emerge' (2016:17)

The second of these cases mapped with my understanding of alternative routes through cities, partly from working as a security guard and navigating spaces outside of customary hours and purposes, but also how routes and locations offered environments for that which they weren't designed (IMT's location was not designed for an art gallery, but, equally appropriately, since 2016 the entrance has become a desirable location for smoking crack). This led to my increased interest in maps laid over each other, and diagrams over maps, and the disorientation of what Burroughs called the 'fold-in': a folding over of a page, using the structure of a book to create new potentialities within the text(s) being folded.

I was more aware of psychogeography through Iain Sinclair (whom I came to from Burroughs) and Alan Moore (whom I came to considerably earlier through comics, first *Halo Jones* and more significantly in *From Hell*) than I was Deleuze and Guattari's deterritorialization and transversality. As such my diagrammatics came through psychogeography as a means of describing the nature of a place not through the logics that place was designed for, but by an experience of moving through it according to different logics. That said, it is just as easy to read these means as attempts at the 'fractures in capitalism' in which Deleuze and Guattari see unconscious imaginings brought into presence through the operations of alternative logics and assemblages of multiplicity (1984). Multiplicity here, or indeed Guattari's 'ontological het-erogeneity' of *Chaosmosis* (Guattari 1995), read in terms of the 'polylogue' (Reilly 2018:30). Haraway's 'infidel heteroglossia' as antithesis of a common language from *A Cyborg Manifesto* is also relevant here (Haraway 1985:101).

My other take away from *Junky*, the fugitive, is connected to relations (communities as well as structures) and also to meaning, perhaps 'meaning' as a process of orientation (Maturana). Burroughs' brief mention gains depth and urgency through the implications of Fred Moten's concept of the fugitive. For Moten, in his critique of Kant, the fugitive is

> a desire for and a spirit of escape and transgression of the proper and the proposed. It's a desire for the outside, for a playing or being outside, an outlaw edge proper to the now always already improper voice or instrument.
>
> (Moten 2018)

Although unlike Burroughs who positions fugitivity as a quality of addicts and jive-talkers, specifically a quality of language, Moten positions it as the oppression of the black imaginary within white supremacist modernity. Whilst Burroughs' fugitivity is about shifted meaning in travel through time and space, for Moten, fugitivity is a state of freedom and unfreedom; a restlessness disruption of structures born from bondage.

Legacy Russell's 2016 IMT exhibition *WANDERING/ Wilding: Blackness on the Internet* pursues with comparable urgency and relevance the implications of such language, with its consideration of Baudelaire's 'roving soul' against '*wilding*', *a* dog-whistle term word which came into mainstream use in 1980s New York used to mark the collective socializing of black and brown bodies as inherent public threat and, in turn, justify increased profiling and policing of such bodies throughout New York City.

I am conscious of appropriating aesthetics and tools of struggle against white supremacy. But these themes and the implications of their unsettled movements: the fugitive (always between states of autonomy and restriction), the virus (always moving in to find a host) are relations that describes a place that holds. We have similar enemies even whilst the violence they inflict upon us is incomparable.

This attempt to describe some of the most focused curatorial intensities that have taken place at the gallery is, I suggest, comparable to the 'barbarism' of the relational (Aiken in Reilly 2018:30). It is not that these intensities are universal in the programme, but that they are recurrent curatorial traits that, though the work of collaborators, allow the holding together of sets of resources that pursue similar means.

This is how we curate virally/relationally/diagrammatically/in grooving/as metamodelization.[12]

When we lose agency, we replace it with ritual. IMT's logo is a sigil. In his 1983 article 'Sorcerous Symbols', chaos magician Phil Hine describes sigils for use in the first edition of *Advanced Dungeons & Dragons* (1983). For Hine, and in the context of the game world, sigils are a form of 'picture-glyph [...] attuned to a specific, wished-for desire. [...] When the sigil is consciously concentrated upon, energy is released from [...] the vast untapped resources of [the user's] subconscious' (ibid. 18). The sigil is trust not in brand recognition and not in the business ontology, but in a different kind of diagram that succeeds or fails on alternative logics. Sigils as devices for calling things into existence. Once an Arts Council England application has been drafted and signed off, we bless the envelope.

The experimentation of curation at IMT is to challenge curatorial control, taking Burroughs' tape praxis in the case of *Dead Fingers Talk* as a means to disturb what Burroughs called 'the cycle of conditioned action' but what in 21st century curatorial anxieties is an internalization of the canon of art history and its faces (including, but not exhaustively, white supremacy, patriarchy, ableism, and the normative influences of the heterosexual matrix) but also in attempt to work with an exhibition in a way that didn't consider art (or indeed artists) as a passive object to be gawked at.[13] Instead exhibition-making as Breakdown describes it: something that can't be synthesized outside of the actual moment, 'you have to find ways of working with it while it is still alive and slippery' (Breakdown 2021, personal communication, 25 October). An engagement at the site of artistic exchange with art, not as an artefact separated from life and reaching towards a substantiation of a past, but as 'a didactic proposition that, through its form, heralds new projects [that] resonate with meaning [through being] a collaboration and future production' (Jackson 2014b:201). I would later understand this through Plastique Fantastique's production–contingency assemblage (substituting my clumsy terms of 'collaboration' for production and 'future production' for contingency). For Burroughs the cut-up was not an object of intrinsic value in its physical manifestation but only in the (artistic mode) of making things happen and the (social mode) of being a call for 'cut-ups are for everyone' (Burroughs and Gysin 1978:31):

> [This book] is not the history of a literary collaboration but rather the complete fusion in a praxis of two subjectivities, two subjectivities that metamorphose into a third; it is from this collusion that a new author emerges, an absent third person, invisible and beyond grasp, decoding the silence.
>
> (ibid. 1978:18)

But the diagram isn't just exhibition-building but superimposed throughout IMT's structures and relations. A diagram superimposed over artworld infrastructures. A hybrid space is one that adopts characteristics of models drawn from both the commercial gallery sector (exclusive representation of artists and participation in art fairs), characteristics normally associated with artist-led or garage spaces (non-profit company structure and projects funded through public bodies) as well as characteristics reminiscent of affiliation with academic teaching and research. This, then, is the hybrid gallery.

Notes

1 Marchart argues that the contemporary biennale is a work of decolonization as 'the global history of the future is being written from today's periphery', though 'the artistic decentralization of the West', Marchart's identification of the biennial's counter-hegemonic shifting of centres. He acknowledges that 'authoritarian regimes utilize the biennial format to glamourize their image and prepare the tourism industry for the post-oil era' (ibid. 24) whilst in agreement with Hou Hanru that 'Biennials are [...] opening up new public spaces for artistic production outside the dominant market' (ibid. 27).

2 It is worth noting also that this concept bears relation to some of the beliefs of the Church of Scientology, not least the ability to exteriorize one's consciousness, especially considering Burroughs' growing affiliation with Dianetics, and thereafter Scientology, during his stay in Tangier.

3 Featuring work by Alma/Joe Ambrose, Steve Aylett, Alex Baker and Kit Poulson, William S. Burroughs, Lawrence English, the Human Separation, Riccardo Iacono, Anthony Joseph, Cathy Lane, Eduardo Navas, Negativland, O. Blaat, Aki Onda, Jörg Piringer, Plastique Fantastique, Simon Reuben White, Giorgio Sadotti, Scanner, Terre Thaemlitz, Thomson and Craighead, Laureana Toledo, and Ultra-red, with live performances by Ascsoms, Joel Cahen, and Solina Hi-Fi, film by Lars Movin and Steen Møller Rasmussen and a series of talks by David Burrows, Mark Jackson, Anthony Joseph, Kit Poulson, David Toop, and Salomé Voegelin, and followed by *Swarms of Black Flies Make the Roses Purple* (2012), with Edwina Ashton, Alex Baker and Kit Poulson, William Burroughs, Brion Gysin, Emma Hart, Alejandro Ospina, and Plastique Fantastique.

4 *Dead Fingers Talking* an audio-only mix of the exhibition featured as part of *Be Glad for the Song Has No End* (2010) at the Wysing Arts Centre, Cambridgeshire, a festival organized and arranged by Andy Holden.

5 *Silencer* with work by Alex Baker, Audio Research Editions, Corrado Morgana and Nye Parry, part of 4by4, a series of exhibitions in association with Neville Brody's The Anti-Design Festival (2010).

6 *Dead Fingers Talk 2012, The Mayan Caper* with work by Alma/ Joe Ambrose, Steve Aylett, Alex Baker, William S. Burroughs and Ian Sommerville, Leslie Deere, Phillip Drummond, Lizzie Hughes, Anthony Joseph, Cathy Lane, Mark Jackson, Duncan McAfee, Eduardo Navas, Charlotte Norwood, Settimio Palermo, Simon Reuben White, Giorgio Sadotti, Scanner, Terre Thaemlitz, Laureana Toledo, and Ultra-red.

7 Hylton's *Nature of the Beast* (2007) is a relevant precursor to Quaintance's summary here.

8 The shortlist being comprised of Array Collective, Black Obsidian Sound System, Cooking Sections, Gentle/Radical, and Project Art Works.

9 The work Skerl is analysing here comes from a period in which Burroughs was categorizing the United States as a matriarchy, and deriding femininity in gay men as a symptom of the sex war. Many of his most problematic statements about gender and sexuality come from this period.

10 Stupart deliberately (and brilliantly in terms of the theme and intent of their text) refuses to reference Burroughs but instead locates language as a virus with Kathy Acker.

11 *Years without Art* (1977–80) later reframed by Stewart Home and the PRAXIS groups as a proposed Art Strike (1990–93).

12 See also Lucy A. Sames who translates diagrammatic practice explicitly and effectively into a curatorial mode (2022).

13 In the exhibition *Snow Crash* Cooke used construction scaffolding to similar ends, with the scaffolding deployed as a material and architecture as a *provisional material* that, for Cooke,

> speculates on what will come into being but is not the fixed resulting site. Therefore, the scaffolding held the tensions and negotiations between myself, as the curator of the exhibition, and the artists in the exhibition. [...] It also draws on the uses of use, which comes from Ahmed [(2019)], centred around the queering of use: Thinking about what we use, to find how we're used.
>
> (Cooke 2022, personal communication, 28 September)

17 Making a Fucking Mess of It

Rohtmaa-Jackson: [reading from an email] ... how do you feel about ... about IMT's programme?

Friend: We make these projects and we put them out, but we never ask anyone if they want them ...

Cooke: Yes, because we produce exhibitions to bring new publics into being, not to show people what they are already familiar with.

(IMT Zoom Meeting 09/08/2022)

IMT's exhibition and event history is erratic, complex, and sometimes contradictory. Early exhibitions of artists that have gone on to acclaim, oddities with collections of non-artists, and artists both emerging and established. Attempting a holistic overview of the gallery's curatorial activities inevitably will produce exceptions and inconsistencies. Rather than merely being indicative of a lack of ideological design, our constant discussion of what IMT is, has, from the start, consciously adopted an experimentalist approach that has rejected conventional theoretical approaches as much as been informed by them. IMT's curatorial activities are as much a hybrid as its structure, ultimately offering a paradoxical consistency. Hence why the hybrid is, in this book, the theme.

As such the problem of writing IMT gallery into criticism: recreating events, scrutinizing practices and structures, and isolating themes, is that large parts of its history contradict or fail consistency. Separating the mouth from the rest of the body is about

DOI: 10.4324/9781003197959-18

suggesting a focus, a particular emphasis of shaping ideas and positioning them in relation to materials. And the tension in curating, and the source of its arrogance, is between imagining a focus and a holisticism, compromising somewhere in an act of *différance*. The gallery is a productive entity led by its experimentalism, but even where this is most clearly articulated and can then be seen to follow through the making-public of exhibitions, there are equally moments where we give up or run out of means. We are not always ideologically coherent, often allow ourselves to be led by our hearts or by chance or by indifference as a positive value (see Roth and Katz 1998:35) and occasionally have to make concessions for our mental and physical health and find a space to act 'without strictness' (Tingle 2022).[1] There are also clearly times when we take on the appearance of normal, legitimate, and dominant models, yet we maintain a persistent relationship to our queerness, often prioritizing 'whatever is at odds with the normal, the legitimate, the dominant [...] a positionality vis-à-vis the normative' (Halperin 1997) as a means to outmanoeuvre our frustrations with present conditions. As Phillips identifies amongst histories of self-organization:

> Our 'value sets' are mixed –they are heterogeneous, contradictory and often politically hostile to each other in the sense that we might value organizational alterity but our governance processes and our fundraising strategies mean working with people whose value sets favor normalization.
>
> (Phillips 2019:298)

Sometimes this tension results in fantasies in which the museum cabinet becomes a wargaming table (see Hughes and Rohtmaa-Jackson 2022) or in the certainty that the neoliberal alienation of the art world can only be articulated through the languages of preppers and survivalists.[2] Ultimately therefore terms like 'unsettled' and 'hybrid', and the transitory connotations of 'holding' feel applicable here. I shall reflect on these terms, especially the hybrid, and consider their course.

Notes

1 'you are too strict and it hurts your body so lets [sic.] have space where you speak without strictness' (Tingle 2022).

2 *Feeling Safer* (2016) an exhibition which drew some of its methodology from O'Doherty's assertion that the white cube gallery represented an ethos in which 'the outside world must not come in' (1999:7) updated to the paranoid and violent Anglo-American imagination that gave us Brexit and Trump.

18 Curatorial Practice

The mouths at the encounter are offensive. COVID has made this explicit: THE ALIEN SALIVA AROUND THE CANDY CARRIES A VIRUS. THE SWEET ON THE FLOOR CARRIES A VIRUS. THE BRAIN. THE TONGUE. THE EGG. THEY CARRY A VIRUS. The virus coming off the page. It leaks up and enters us in some way that makes us have to reconfigure our relationship to the environment. Dancing. Grooving. Saying hello. '[Disconnecting] the concept of reality [...] imposed on us and then [plugging] normally disassociated zones into the same sector' (Burroughs and Gysin 1987:17). We stick our tongues under fascist skin.

IMT is a project. IMT forever temporary, and it burns. IMT is reading Ray Bradbury's *The Martian Chronicles*. An automated house burns to the ground. All of the automated tasks keep going through the blaze, but with a series of voices wailing 'Fire! Fire! Run! Run!' to long gone inhabitants, fading as the wires popped their sheaths like hot chestnuts. In this story the fire is clever and makes its way up to the house's attic brain, whilst one divergent automated voice reads randomly selected poetry aloud in the fiery study, 'until all the film-spools burned, until all the wires withered and the circuits cracked' (1951:168–9).

That this type of hybrid co-opting is almost childish. When I come across the toys of my own child, it is not whole toys that speak of their world, it is the parts of toys. The bottom half of an empty container is a car wheel. A ball without its racket is an ice cream. A plate, removed from its picnic set, is a biscuit. Orphaned, co-opted, and fictioned into an assemblage of world nested, a

DOI: 10.4324/9781003197959-19

diagram of relations, at an angle to my world of laptops and coffee makers. What became clear in the living and working of the gallery is that it is an organism that lives in expectation of its dismantling. Its mouths snap at morsels from different ecosystems and attach themselves to passers-by, but it is a hypervisible fugitive in fear of being seen and torn up. I have written about the curatorial practice that is IMT as a hybrid with the aim of contributing to thinking about curatorial practice.

IMT is a basin that holds things. Its hybridity and unsettledness in a post-2010 funding environment means it is implicitly always in a state of need. As such all projects and activities become means to its desires: a research project will be built around a financial service to IMT; the compromise of time spent elsewhere will always also need to feed it somehow. I felt that I personally, beyond my identity wrapped up in IMT's Third, wanted to do things that had their own orbit and break IMT's holding.

We are ever in search of the critical. Yet all the practices and structures described in this book are attempts to find routes by which criticality can be negotiated. Our use of the unsettled, of the hybrid, and the things that manifest through its intervention, is to investigate what art-making, exhibition-making, gallery-making was at the point at which IMT appeared.

IMT offers itself as a vessel, and open mouth, a Walk-in. This is partly the enjoyment of all galleries that resist coherence, but for IMT it is deliberate. Yet the gallery is not open. Part of its hybridity, its secret, is that it is the home of Friend and of the cats: Cordelia, Walter, and Madge. IMT has an intimacy that is sacred; a series of hazy thresholds. The cats ensure the gallery is never empty, even when Friend is out its hallway and rooms still traversed when the door is locked and the art is lived *with*.

IMT as an attempt to work through territorialization, to see more clearly the infrastructures that existed in the fields we were moving through. O'Sullivan outlines this in 'On the Diagram (and a Practice of Diagrammatics)' in his description of metamodelization and the diagram. O'Sullivan describes this as a tool that is both a 'strategic and pragmatic [...] bringing together of different models', and how the diagram is a way of 're-positioning existing frameworks, and of working out possible relations as well as divergences'. For O'Sullivan this allows practices that reject 'the way things are, [opening] up thought to other perspectives and points of view' (2016:20)

Our formulations of IMT, as exemplified by curatorial design, involve this metamodelization, from Guattari, a collage of diagrams from extreme mechanics which artists, curators, and galleries might navigate the spaces that they find themselves in. The hybrid is born from this. Metamodelization as a production of alternative models. This is the fifth mouth at work.

Burrows and O'Sullivan give a succinct description of metamodelization in the introduction to *Fictioning,* tying metamodelization to fictioning as an example of 'theory into practice' (2019:8), a refusal of 'any partisanship or single philosophic dogma'. Burrows and O'Sullivan go into significant detail about the implications of such practices in the context of their practice, but their Promethean concept of placing 'the pathemic and mathemic [...] in dialogue' (ibid. 353) and how this follows John Mullarkey's 'meta-philosophical diagram' as 'an infinite set of materialised "betweens"' (ibid. 359n) is useful here. Returning to Friend's construct of the artist-as-business and the (*Space Hulk*) hybrid as a creature, here we are proposing a fugitive Prometheus that is also between the animal (patheme) and the formal (matheme).

How do we operate in the hostile (Phillips) conditions of the void and its own hybrid infrastructure made from the mystical discharges of capitalism, and not be coded by it? Ancelin-Bourguignon et al. (2019) propose a 'transferability thesis' as a means of transferring artistic and creative practices from art-makers to the business sector (of which the art world is undeniably a part). For them however it is clear that transferability is severely restricted by management's resistance to changes that do not adhere to the spirit of capitalism, instead serving only to 'make capitalism more attractive' (2019:39). Add to this Russell's discussion of the problems of mimicry, describing how artists and arts organizations are complicit in their similarity to and reliance on corporate structures, but with additional questions around the art world's lack of supervision and accountability (2022:143–6). Cooke's answer, both for their own curatorial practice and for IMT, is to 'rewire [these infrastructures] and give a space for different voices and technological systems to emerge' (Cooke 2022, personal communication, 28 September). A recoding of contemporary gallery infrastructures, or, as Cooke sees the work we do, as a constant asking of the question, 'we are always fictioning our interactions with the world, how do we fiction them differently?'

We need to tell different stories. This is what keeps us together, storytelling. We are the act of giving space to different stories.

This being the case, what claims does the gallery make for artists? For audiences? For community whether local or global? For a history or histories of cultural activity? Do these claims of the *between* hold up as convincing? I have described how a hybrid approach to repurposing comes via William Burroughs, or via Easterling, and for AAS in the idea of the 'trickster organisation' via Hansen. These are the thoughts behind how we use our tongues to deposit an egg within a fascist infrastructure (body), an egg that takes properties from multiple systems, an egg 'traversed by gradients marking the transitions and the becomings, the destinations of the subject developing along these particular vectors' (Deleuze and Guattari 1984:19).[1]

This is a book about mouths, and swallowing is its end. As such this book is an archival gesture, as O'Sullivan puts it, 'a framing and presenting of a subset of the world' (2014). Following O'Sullivan, this book is then curatorial whilst also being about curating. O'Sullivan continues: 'crucially, it does not necessarily transform these elements [but] offers nothing more than a product [...] designed to meet the desire for knowledge [...] of the world as-it-is'. There is of course an argument for a book like this being exactly that. The satisfaction of desire to know something as-it-is or was. But I would argue that that is not what this book is most useful for. In conversation with Lasse Høgenhof about the LungA Art School in Seyðisfjörður, he describes LungA as a project that in other sites may instead be recognizable as 'kiosks [...] cafes [...] a library [...] a chess club' (Høgenhof 2022, personal communication 21 March) and that is part of how I have tried to make my gestures. And hopefully it is the weak points of this archive, at which this gesture is illegible or confused in some way, where I have tried to break through its subject, where I have tried to make this not just a paraphrasing of a praxis (for it should have been clear that IMT is unarguably a praxis) and not just 'the *feel* of something different' (O'Sullivan 2014:4) but also something alien, that 'performs its own alienation [...] from and for an already alienated subject' (ibid. 9).

I did talk of aliens that are already fixed in the world as-it-is, the hybrid of *Space Hulk* may be a postmodern construction but with a relatively clear ancestry in politics, comics, and popular horror cinema, and the Visitors of Strieber are built though similar means from different building blocks, but it is the points at which these aliens are perhaps more banal that makes them truly odd. And it is the abject qualities of the sticky candy from the mouth of the alien that is the real consistency of alienation through which IMT might, as I have drawn it, have managed to escape its archive, or at least have writhed enough to loosen the archival gesture's hold.

So this book is about how IMT remains unsettled and inconsistent. How its hybridity is an attempt to find a place from which art's aims of originality, and the social implications of those aims, can be negotiated. As Cooke succinctly described it in a conversation over Zoom in December of 2021: 'We choose to be inconsistent because we want difference in the world'. In this book, I have shown how hybrid organization and management of IMT has produced its functioning and survival, but also how they have continuously been contested into an unsettled state.

And it is hopefully clear here that this text suggests that it is important that the hybrids proliferate. That they don't merely appear as maquettes of the big institutions who pride themselves on global visibility and industrialize how they financially sustain themselves. That they don't merely justify and scaffold the art market and the art fair complex and the convivial parties of Venice. That they don't merely act as vanity to those artists with access to space to give their personal projects context but also allow themselves criticality and conflict.

So, my starting principles with IMT as curatorial practice, reaching as close as I got to a sustained articulation of it, was via Burroughs. And of course, as I think I remember being warned by Angus Carlyle at some point early on: Burroughs was wrong. The brain isn't a computer. The world we experience isn't a movie. But the further I get from that point and the more our 'memories' are recorded as audio-visual clips in such programs as Facebook and replayed to us as memories, the more we try to replicate Burroughs' delusion, the more we believe in such a God, the more it brings the OGU into existence. The organization and archiving of culture in the white cube of the gallery space feels like this process. Its hybridity, Burroughsian in its cut-and-paste cybernetics, is internecine. It is not a solution but an attempt to reveal places from which a solution can be negotiated. Always this. And IMT's trajectory from this point, moving digital residencies and peda-gogical experiments, maintains this unsettled searching.

Simply put, IMT, as a project, was for us a Burroughsian space: an always temporary space of potential that was similarly unreachable. But through experimental cutting-up of pre-existing materials we might reveal the point from which such space might be negotiated. As such, it was for us a multitude and machine whose unsettled outline made possible a collective production of desire. It was a thing that we gave naive form: *art gallery*, and then quickly grew to understand how such forms must then form themselves where they are left ill-defined. And crucially that if this becoming is not guided or intervened in then it may click into pre-existing structures and tendencies which are, for the most part, exploitative and violent. So, we twist this space and tickle it to make it laugh and make it stoned and move it around in our mouths, learning it and reshaping it until it disappears and is replenished. And we share the space, half-sucked, with others each time it is unready to be shared.

The business imaginaries of artist-led gallery practice have produced an enduring awkwardness in their relation to the various industries of art and art's entanglement with the money nexus. Negative understandings of gallery and curatorial practice have become entrenched through the making visible of the infrastructures that regulate contemporary art practices. Rather than considering the commercial gallery and the non-profit gallery to be opposing models of gallery practice, we have reasoned through our work that it might be more honest, useful, and representative of the practices that surround us to develop understanding of these conditions as relational. Neither commercial nor non-profit activities and objects are absolute, neither are those who lead such spaces inde-pendent, as highlighted by galleries operating more definitively in either domain borrowing from each other or depending in some way on the other's success for their modelling. These conditioning relationalities draw attention to the multiplicities of art practice for artists and audiences and the potential for developing more sophisticated approaches to how these things interact.

As these methods are becoming more common, even visible in major international organizations and curated events, it is becoming clear that they are not answers in and of themselves. But they do address key issues: corporate alienation among them.

From some of the texts here and the ideas: horizontalism, collaboration, antagonism towards the money nexus, one could assume this is intrinsically an attempt to be a solution. But this argument isn't a redemptive reading of art and exhibition-making. All these modes remain unsettled; the horizontal remains a confluence of gradients, of peaks and troughs. This is a text that sets itself apart from the materiality of its practice yet attempts to smudge it. Held in the mouth whilst you work, stopping you from talking, reminding you that you are a body.

So IMT as a thing is, to us, nothing but what it will be. This is IMT at the point of starting these chapters. And it is evident that the unsettled nature of the gallery is its fragility, especially in an environment of pandemic emergencies and the political vandalism of right-wing Tory populism that is seeking the dismantling of cultural bodies that it can't control. So as IMT, as a thing, is nothing but what it will be, and that being is on the verge of its extinction, is IMT an angel? Possibly. It is a thing that holds, for now.

In this book I have tried to craft something that is closer to the facts of perception than a more decisively structured text would allow. I hope I haven't tried your patience and given you something that drifts in an unsettled manner around the edges of creativity and utility (Ancelin-Bourguingon et al. 2019).

O'Sullivan describes fictioning, in part, via his reading of Burroughs, as a transformative 'deployment of other times in the present' (O'Sullivan in Gunkel et al. 2017:6). Burroughs' activities with such deployment extend from the cut-up technique to the displacement or introduction of incongruous characters and settings, especially those taken from or inspired by sci-fi, fantasy and folklore themes and literary genres. This deployment, to use O'Sullivan's phrase, is applied by Burroughs as a method of escaping an impasse of a linear time, causality, and destiny maintained by social control and addiction. For Burroughs this is an externally enforced system for maintaining a planetary condition (such as population control and societal divisions as well as biological and behavioural conventions). IMT follows a similar trajectory. We constructed a world from past, present, and future resources to deploy variably as a social tool, a world-building exercise, or a desired alternative to present conditions.

Note

1 It might be clear that the Body without Organs is a key reference point here, as it is also a key influence on *The Cult of Possible Elements*, an artwork-as-exhibition by AAS that is described earlier. But I take a scenic route via the hybrids of *Space Hulk* not just because it's scenic but because it's closer to the truth. The egg on the tongue, an egg that is also a candy and a sliver of preserved brain, is an image folded into this representation of an art gallery called IMT.

19   Five Mouths Reprise

Why and how was it useful to think about mouths? A series of mouths that aren't just for creating words?

The candy in the mouth, like the project, eventually ceases to exist. When we code a model like this one, as John Russell claims for fictioning, 'the end retro-codes the story backwards from the end' (Russell 2009:83). The lingering taste of the candy, lining the whole of the mouth, conceals the bodily switch between Visitor and writer.

IMT hasn't ended for me writing this, even though its project status establishes an eventual end in its beginning. So, the coding here is not from the end, but from where we are going now. The intensities in this text have histories that stretch back to IMT's beginnings but are the ones offered up because they are moving forward to some point between now and the end.

The Visitor's candy in Streiber's mouth tastes of science fiction, alien abduction, missing time and lack of control over one's own body. It seems fervently on the side of artistic discourse. Then he hears the voice of the visitor for the first time, goes into a panic, and rampages around the house with a loaded gun. The Visitor never returns. Candy is also a stand in for addiction. When Chris Farley joked about shooting pains on Letterman in 1996, Letterman jokes 'maybe you should cut back on the candy'. Farley was to die the following year at the age of 33 from an overdose of cocaine and morphine.

Thus, candy is more of a cultural than a natural object. It may have once been made by hand but now is part of the mass

DOI: 10.4324/9781003197959-20

production of capitalism. A particularly engineered experience of aesthetics and taste.

In their book *In the Dream House*, Machado speaks as a visitor, not as a curator. In the mausoleum of the gallery away from the street they are a consumer of culture. They don't include in their account the choice the artist gives to the owner of the work: whether the candy is replenished. As such an exhibition may see Ross disappear or may see them revived daily. Sweets likewise are respawned in the shops they come from, tasting the same as they did when we first ate them. Steven Connor suggests sweets are magical objects with 'a collective mythology' (2011:199). A Jungian collective memory makes the job of the curator significantly easier. It is a solitary act that makes us think we have time to play. It is cute. Irresponsible. It is a tiny, almost meaningless, revolt against biopower: an up yours to the health matrix. We know they are bad for us, that they each present a risk to our fragile bodies, whether their shape, their longevity, or their collection of teeth, but they are a temporary relief; a tiny, internal carnival. And the eating of sweets, for Connor, evokes a threshold: 'sweets and sweetness are the essence of eating. But this is why we do not want to swallow sweetness, because we know that swallowing is its end' (ibid. 199).

In Machado's story the movement of a candy in the mouth takes two people and a pile of sweets in an art gallery and turns it into three people, becomes a multitude of Felix, Ross, a brother? A family. A history of politics, exclusion, memory, forgetting, social and personal violence. How can a room containing sweets house all this complexity and not fall apart? What is the holding pattern that keeps the gallery at a minimal consistency without erasing this complexity? In this book the candy is a quasi-object moving around the mouth and around which I am building an image of IMT.

When I first officially asked Friend if we could have a recorded conversation about IMT for this book I asked her what she thought IMT was. She replied, 'IMT is my dream'. And it *is* a dream space. A dream space that persists as long as a candy sliver remains in the mouth. And I see this in Friend in Burroughsian terms as, 'a world forever being reshuffled in the mind, a world that belongs to oneself like the contents of a dream' (Kazin in Murphy 1997:142). If it is anything more than this, IMT is an organization of tools that allows a shared dream to maintain its existence.

The problem with the unsettled is there is no defined aim, no consistent area of concern, no result. IMT's mode is not a social solution but entangles social concerns in its existence as, in its most basic form, a collaboration around transience. A third mouth, carrying traces of former architectures, directing the host towards texts on bardo. A holding. Without solutions other than a motivation to redirect money to artists as well as create opportunities for sharing, whilst helping steer artists' labour away from the debts and obligations that underlie capitalism.

This book isn't about a gallery that exists or ever existed. This book is a sweet, sucked to try and remember what a gallery is. This book is about a creative process being gradually sucked away to reveal nothing but a lingering taste. What IMT might be. It is as close and as far away as that. In Iggy Pop's *Candy* (1990), he sings about the memory of a lost love. As materiality disperses in our mouths, our minds fabricate a beneficent god.[1] Paying rent, in the building, we are the things I have mentioned. We are in our roles with it, within this space and its proliferation of mouths, aware of the various contrary positions we take: Artist–curator. Colleague–kin. Author–vessel. Killer–healer. The temporariness of a candy. Its thin shell collapsing to reveal a liquid centre.

Note

1 Deleuze and Guattari 1988:3.

20 Ends

Three mouths, the second, third, and fourth, describe their shared dream:

I met a dead friend. We hugged – a pattern recognition. He told me he couldn't eat eggs. He took me to meet an old technician who struggled to remember me, and we set up a stand offering games of jackstones before a great wooden door that led out of the city.[1]

Note

1 Rohtmaa-Jackson, M. [dream] Gateshead, 29 July 2022.

DOI: 10.4324/9781003197959-21

References

Abercrombie, N. and Longhurst, B. (1998) *Audiences*. London: Sage.

Ahmed, S. (2006) *Queer Phenomenology*. Durham: Duke.

Ahmed, S. (2019) *What's the Use?* Durham: Duke.

Ancelin-Bourguignon, A., Dorsett, C. and Azambuja, R. (2019) 'Lost in Translation? Transferring Creativity Insights from Arts into Management', *Organisation*, June 2019. 27.5. pp. 717–41.

Attali, J. (1977) *Noise: The Political Economy of Music*. Minneapolis: Minnesota.

Barthes, R. (1977) 'The Death of the Author', in Heath, S. (ed.) *Image Music Text*. London: Fontana, pp. 142–8

Baudrillard, J. (1996) 'Disneyworld Company', *Libération*, March 4. Available: https://archis.org/volume/disneyworld-company/ (Accessed 4 January 2023).

Baudrillard, J. (1976) *Symbolic Exchange and Death*. London: Sage. 1993

Beech, D. (2010) 'Weberian Lessons: Art, Pedagogy and Managerialism' in O'Neill, P. and Wilson, M. (eds.) *Curating and the Educational Turn*, London: Open Editions, pp. 47–60.

Bishop, C. (2012) *Artificial Hells: Participatory Art and the Politics of Spectatorship*. London: Verso.

Black, J. (1926) *You Can't Win*. New York: Macmillan.

Black Swan (2022a) 'Black Swan Speaks', in Catlow, R. and Rafferty, P. (eds.) *Radical Friends*. London: Torque Editions, pp. 280–1.

Black Swan (2022b) 'Cygnet Prototype', in Catlow, R. and Rafferty, P. (eds.) *Radical Friends*. London: Torque Editions, pp. 322–5.

Blamey, D. (ed.) (2016) *Specialism*. London: Open Editions.

Boltanski, L. and Chiapello, E. (1999) *The New Spirit of Capitalism*. London: Verso. 2005.

Bourdieu, P. (1979) *Distinction: A Social Critique of the Judgement of Taste*. Cambridge: Harvard. 1986.

Bradbury, N. (2013) 'Paulette Terry Brien of the International 3'. *Corridor8*. 23 September. Available: https://corridor8.co.uk/article/interview-paule tte-terry-brien-of-international-3/ (Accessed 17 March 2022).

Bradbury, R. (1951) *The Martian Chronicles*. London: Harper.

Burroughs, W. (1986a) *The Adding Machine*. New York: Seaver.

Burroughs, W. (1986b) *Break Through in Grey Room*. Vinyl. Sub Rosa.

Burroughs, W. (2003) *Junky*. New York: Penguin Books.

Burroughs, W. (1964) *Nova Express*. New York: Grove. 1992.

Burroughs, W. (1985) *Queer*. London: Picador, 1986.

Burroughs, W. and Gysin, B. (1978) *The Third Mind*. London: John Calder. 1979.

Burroughs, W. Jr. (2006) *Cursed from Birth: The Short, Unhappy Life of William S. Burroughs, Jr*. New York: Soft Skull.

Burrows, D. and O'Sullivan, S. (2019) *Fictioning: The Myth-Functions of Contemporary Art and Philosophy*. Edinburgh University.

Burrows, D. and O'Sullivan, S. (2014) 'The Sinthome/Z-Point Relation or Art as Non-Schizoanalysis', in Buchanan, I. and Collins, L. (eds.) *Deleuze and the Schizoanalysis of Visual Art*. London: Bloomsbury, pp. 253–78.

Butt, G. (2005) *Between You and Me*. Durham: Duke.

Catlow, R. and Garrett, M. (2021) Artgames and interspecies LARPS. 3 November. Available: https://soundcloud.com/reimaginevalue/furtherfi eld (Accessed 23 October 2022).

Catlow, R., Garrett, M., Jones, N. and Skinner, S. (eds.) (2017) *Artists Re: Thinking the Blockchain*. London: Torque Editions.

Catlow, R. and Rafferty, P. (eds.) (2022) *Radical Friends*. London: Torque Editions.

Cohen, J. (2020) 'Notes from the Cave: Searching for Prophecy in the Midst of a Pandemic', *Bookforum*, June/July/August. Available: www. bookforum.com/print/2702/searching-for-prophecy-in-the-midst-of-a-pandemic-24017 (Accessed 3 September 2022).

Connor, S. (2011) *Paraphernalia: The Curious Lives of Magical Things*. London: Profile.

Cussans, J. (2017) *Undead Uprising*. London: Strange Attractor.

Deleuze, G. (1985) *Cinema 2: The Time-Image*. London: Athlone. 1989.

Deleuze, G. (2003) *Francis Bacon: The Logic of Sensation*. London: Continuum.

Deleuze, G. and Burroughs, W. (1969) 'Mother and I Would Like to Know'. *The Evergreen Review*. June.

Deleuze, G. and Guattari, F. (1984) *Anti-Oedipus: Capitalism and Schizophrenia*. London: Athlone.

Deleuze, G. and Guattari, F. (1988) *A Thousand Plateaus: Capitalism and Schizophrenia*. London: Athlone. 1999.

Doussan, J. (2013) 'Eros, Plague, Olfaction: Three Allegories of the Curatorial', in Martinon, J. (ed.) *The Curatorial*. London: Bloomsbury, pp. 79–89.

Easterling, K. (2016) *Extrastatecraft: The Power of Infrastructure Space*. London: Verso.

Ellison, R. (1952) *Invisible Man*. New York: Random House.

Enns, A. (2004) 'Burroughs's Writing Machines' in Schneiferman, D. and Walsh, P. (eds.) *Retaking the Universe: William Burroughs in the Age of Globalization*. London: Pluto, pp. 95–115.

Fernández, M. (2009) '"Life-like": Historicizing Process and Responsiveness in Digital Art', in Preziosi (ed.) *The Art of Art History*. Oxford: Oxford University, pp. 468–487.

The Evil of the Daleks (1967). Directed by Derek Matinus (1967) and AnneMarie Walsh (2021). [Blu-ray, BBCBD0531]. London: BBC. 2021

Feveractal (2021) *Plastique Fantastique Gathering for Speaking and Show*. 26 March, Northumbria University, Newcastle upon Tyne.

Foucault, M. (1984) *The History of Sexuality Volume 2: The Use of Pleasure*. London: Penguin Books. 1992.

Finkelpearl, T. (2001) *Dialogues in Public Art*. Cambridge: MIT.

Fisher, M. (2009) *Capitalist Realism*. London: Zero.

Fisher, M. (2018) *k-punk*. London: Repeater.

Fitzgerald, F. (1926) *All the Sad Young Men*. New York: Charles Scribner's Sons.

Friday 13th Part V: A New Beginning (1985). Directed by Danny Steinmann. [DVD, EC 101042]. Paramount. 2002.

George, A. (2015) *The Curator's Handbook*. London: Thames & Hudson.

Gilbert, J. (2004) 'Becoming Music: The Rhizomic Moment of Improvisation', in Buchanan, I. and Swiboda, M. (eds.) *Deleuze and Music*. Edinburgh: Edinburgh University, pp. 118–39.

Grauerholz, J. (2002) 'The Death of Joan Vollmer Burroughs: What Really Happened' *Lawrence.com*.

Green, M. (1991) *The Dream at the End of the World*. New York: HarperCollins.

Grodach, C. (2009) 'Art Spaces, Public Space, and the Link to Community Development'. *Community Development Journal*, October 2010. 45.4, pp. 474–93.

Groys, B. (2009) 'Comrades of Time', *e-flux journal*, December.

Guattari, F. (1995) *Chaosmosis*. Bloomington: Indiana.

Gunkel, H., Hameed, A. and O'Sullivan, S. (eds.) (2017) *Futures & Fictions*. London: Repeater.

Halliwell, R. (1989) *Space Hulk* (board game). Nottingham: Games Workshop.

Halperin, D. (1997) *Saint Foucault: Towards a Gay Hagiography*. Austin: Texas.

Hansen, G. (2001) *The Trickster and the Paranormal*. Bloomington: Xlibris.

The Happiness Patrol (1988) BBC1. 2–16 November.

Haraway, D. (1985) 'A Cyborg Manifesto', *Socialist Review* 80. pp. 65–108.

Harney, S. and Moten, F. (2013) *The Undercommons: Fugitive Planning & Black Study*. London: Minor Compositions.

Harris, J. (ed.) (2004) *Art, Money, Parties*. Liverpool: Liverpool University.

Harris, O. (2003) *William Burroughs and the Secret of Fascination*. Carbondale: Southern Illinois.

Hester, H. (2018) *Xenofeminism*. Cambridge: Polity.

High School Musical 2 (2007). Directed by Kenny Ortega. Available: Disney+ (Accessed 3 May 2020).

Hill, N. (1937) *Think and Grow Rich*. Meriden: Raston.

Hine, P. (1995) *Condensed Chaos*. Tempe: Falcon.

Hine, P. (1983) 'Sorcerous Symbols', *White Dwarf* # 41. May. pp. 18–19.

Hughes, A. and Rohtmaa-Jackson, M. (2022) 'Citadel of Chaos: An Art Practice to Materialise an Alternate Present', in *Vector*. Available: https:// vector-bsfa.com/2022/08/24/citadel-of-chaos-an-art-practice-to-mate rialise-an-alternate-present/ (Accessed 24 August 2022).

Hughes, A. and Jackson, M. (2018) '*Polymorph Other: Thursday 5 April 5–9 pm*' media release, 29 March, London: IMT Gallery.

Hylton, R. (2007) *The Nature of the Beast*. Bath: ICIA.

ICA (2016) *Technology Now: Blackness on the Internet*. ICA London, UK, 16 November.

Illich, I. (1971) *Deschooling Society*. London: Calder and Boyars.

IMT (2012) *Henrik Schrat|Report on Probability B at IMT Gallery|21st September–21st October 2012*, media release, 11 September, London: IMT.

IMT Gallery (2021) 'IMT Manifesto 4.0 WIP', in Robertson, S. (ed.) *A Manifesto of Sorts*. Brighton: Fifthsyllable, pp. 50–53.

Jackson, M. (2010) *Dead Fingers Talk*. Dazed Digital. 9 July. Accessible at: www.dazeddigital.com/artsandculture/article/7899/1/dead-fingers-talk (Accessed 2 August 2022).

Jackson, M. (2014a) *Alternative 13: Of Doughnut Forms and Meat Patty Forms*. London: IMT.

Jackson, M. (2014b) *Nothing Short of Complete Liberation: The Burroughsian Ideal of Space as Curatorial Strategy in Audial Art*. PhD thesis. University of the Arts London.

Jackson, M. (2014c) *This Is a Game Called 'Hello, Hello, Here Is X.X.'* Vinyl. Laura Palookaville.

Jay, M. (1993) *Downcast Eyes*. Berkeley: California.

Johnson, R. (2006) *The Lost Years of William S. Burroughs: Beats in South Texas*. College Station: Texas A&M.

Jury, S., Kaplinsky, H. and Sames, L. (eds.) (2018) *Alembic*. London: AND.

Kerényi, K. (1943) *Hermes, der Seelenführer* (Hermes: Guide of Souls). Putnum: Spring. 1995.

Kraus, C. (2018) *Social Practices*. South Pasadena: Semiotext(e).

Latour, B. (1991) *We Have Never Been Modern*. Cambridge: Harvard. 1993.

Le Guin, U. (1971) *Lathe of Heaven*. New York: Avon.

Lefebvre, H. (1991) *The Production of Space*. Hoboken: Wiley-Blackwell.

Lewis, J. (ed.) (2001) *Odd Gods: New Religions & the Cult Controversy*. Amherst: Prometheus.

Lotringer, S. (ed.) (1978) *Schizoculture*. South Pasadena: Semiotext(e). 2013.

Luckhurst, R. (2015) Zombies: A Cultural History. London: Reaktion.

Lungs Project (2022) *About*. Available: www.lungsproject.org/about (Accessed 4 May 2022).

Machado, C. (2020) *In the Dream House*. London: Serpent's Tail.

Maleuvre, D. (1999) *Museum Memories: History, Technology, Art*. Redwood City: Stanford.

Marchart, O. (2020) 'The Globalization of Art and the Biennials of Resistance: A History of the Biennials from the Periphery', *OnCurating*, 46, pp. 22–29. June.

Martinon, J. (ed.) (2013) *The Curatorial: A Philosophy of Curating*. London: Bloomsbury.

McKinnon, L. (2022) 'Playing to Extinction: Attention Narcosis and the Hetero-Capitalist Gaze', *Umbigo Magazine*, issue 81.

McLuhan, M. (1964) *Understanding Media*. New York: New American Library.

McLuhan, M. and Fiore, Q. (1967) *The Medium Is the Massage: An Inventory of Effects*. London: Penguin.

Milevska, S. (2013) 'Becoming-Curator', in Martinon, J. (ed.) *The Curatorial*. London: Bloomsbury, pp. 65–71.

Montgomery, R. (1979) *Strangers Among Us*. New York: Fawcett Crest.

Morgan, B. (ed.) (2012) *Rub Out the Words: The Letters of William S Burroughs 1959–1974*. London: Penguin.

Moten, F. (2018) *Stolen Life*. Durham: Duke.

Murphy, S. (2010) *The Art Kettle*. London: Zero.

Murphy, T. (1997) *Wising up the Marks*. Berkeley: California.

Obrist, H. (2014) *Ways of Curating*. London: Penguin.

Oldenburg, R. (1989) *The Great Good Place*. Boston: Da Capo.

O'Doherty, B. (1999) *Inside the White Cube*. Berkeley: California.

O'Neill, P. (2012) *The Culture of Curating and the Curating of Culture(s)*. Cambridge: MIT.

O'Sullivan, S. (2014) 'Art Practice as Fictioning (or, myth-science)', *diakron*, No. 1, online journal (www.diakron.dk), June.

O'Sullivan, S. (2016) 'On the Diagram (and a Practice of Diagrammatics)', in Schneider, K. and Yasar, B. (eds.) *Situational Diagram*. New York: Dominique Lévy, pp. 13–25.

Penda's Fen (1974). Directed by Alan Clarke. [Blu-ray, BFIB1222]. London: BFI. 2016.

Phillips, A. (2019) 'Critical Production, or, the Intelligence of Collective Technicity', in Ana, T. (ed.)*Art Encounters Biennial Catalogue.* Timişoara: Art Encounters, pp. 297–304.

Poole, L. (ed.) (2021) *Phigital*, LUVA/LDVA Gallery zine, June 2021.

Quaintance, M. (2015) *Teleology and the Turner Prize*, e-flux conversations. December. Available: https://conversations.e-flux.com/t/teleology-and-the-turner-prize-or-utility-the-new-conservatism/2936 (Accessed 6 January 2022).

Quaintance, M. (2020a) 'Look Back in Anger', *Art Monthly*, December–January. pp. 6–9.

Quaintance, M. (2020b) 'Remote Viewing', *Art Monthly*, June. pp. 6–9.

Quaintance, M. (2021) 'Look Back in Anger: Part II', *Art Monthly*, February. pp. 11–17.

Raicovich, L. (2021) *Culture Strike*. London: Verso.

Raunig, G. (2013) *Factories of Knowledge Industries of Creativity*. South Pasadena: Semiotext(e).

Reilly, M. (2018) *Curatorial Activism: Towards and Ethics of Curating.* London: Thames & Hudson.

Renton, A. and Gillick, L (1991) *Technique Anglaise: Current Trends in British Art*. London: Thames & Hudson.

Resch, M. (2021) *How to Become a Successful Artist*. London: Phaidon.

Resch, M. (2018) *Management of Art Galleries* (third edition). London: Phaidon.

Robakowski, J. (1977) Catalogue text for the exhibition *Zapisy mechaniczno-biologiczne*, 1978, Warsaw: Mała Galeria PSP-ZPAF.

Rohtmaa-Jackson, M. (2023) *All I Can See Is Trees*, media release, 10 January, London: IMT. Available: https://imagemusictext.com/exhibit ion-all-i-can-see-is-trees/ (Accessed 11 January 2023).

Rohtmaa-Jackson, M. (2020) *This Is a Not-Me launches Thursday 6 August 6–9 pm BST on Twitch + Instagram!*, media release, 31 July, London: IMT. Available: https://imagemusictext.com/exhibition-this-is-a-not-me/ (Accessed 4 January 2023).

Roth, M. and Katz, J. (1998) *Difference/Indifference*. Amsterdam: G+ B Arts.

Russell, J. (2009) 'A Largely Intolerable Combination of Two Mainly Unconnected Texts' in Russell, J. Rowlands, A. and Beasley, M. (eds.) *Barefoot in the Head*. Birmingham: Article, pp. 68–85.

Russell, L. (2022) 'Beauty and the Beast: Collectivity and the Cooporation', in Catlow, R. and Rafferty, P. (eds.) *Radical Friends*. London: Torque Editions, pp. 138–49.

Russell, L. (2020) *Glitch Feminism*. London: Verso.

Sames, L (2022) *Wet Rest: excess as liquid praxis in art and curating*. PhD thesis. Northumbria.

Schrat, H. (2003) 'Feedback', *Art Monthly*, February. pp. 14–15.

Schrat, H. (2002) *The Manager*. Available: https://archiv.henrikschrat.de/2002/feedingback%20new/The%20Manager.htm (Accessed 13 February 2022).

Serres, M. (1977) *The Birth of Physics*. London: Clinamen. 2001.

Serres, M. (1985) *The Five Senses*. London: Continuum. 2008.

Serres, M. (1982) *The Parasite*. Minneapolis: Minnesota. 2007.

Shani, T. (2022) *Why the artworld must stand with Palestine*. Available: https://artreview.com/why-the-artworld-must-stand-with-palestine/ (Accessed 21 March 2022).

Sharon, B. (1979) 'Artist-Run Galleries – A Contemporary Institutional Change in the Visual Arts', *Qualitative Sociology* 2. pp. 3–28.

Skerl, J. (1984) 'Freedom through Fantasy in the Recent Novels of William S. Burroughs', *The Review of Contemporary Fiction* 4.1. pp. 124–30.

Slager, H. (2015). 'Academy as Exhibition' in Wilson, M. and P. O'Neill, P. (eds.) *Curating Research*. London: Open Editions, pp. 79–87.

Soja, E. (1996) *Thirdspace*. Malden: Blackwell, 1996.

Solanas, V. (1971) *SCUM Manifesto*. London: Verso. 2004.

Sollfrank, C. and Stalder, F. (eds.) (2021) *Aesthetics of the Commons*. Zurich: Diaphanes.

Steeds, L. (2016) 'What Is the Future of Exhibition Histories?', in O'Neill, P., Wilson, M. and Steeds, L. (eds.) *The Curatorial Conundrum*. Cambridge: MIT, pp. 17–25.

Steryll, H. (2012) *The Wretched of the Screen*. London: Sternberg.

Streiber, W. (1995) *Breakthrough*. New York: HarperCollins.

Stupart, L. (2016) *Virus*. London: Arcadia Missa.

Suchin, P. (2002) 'Campus Capitalism', *Art Monthly*, September. p. 45.

Sutcliffe, J. (2021) *Documents of Contemporary Art: Magic*. London: Whitechapel Gallery and MIT.

Tatham, J. and O'Sullivan, T. (2013) *Amongst Other Things an Unsuccessful Proposal for the 2012 Cultural Olympiad*. Glasgow: CCA.

Tingle, C. (2022) *BUT i have grown past this. (this is why some spelling mistakes are important for chuck to leave). 'there is no perfect because it is all perfect' has changed my life. way of saying 'you are too strict and it hurts your body so lets have space where you speak without strictness.'* Twitter. 21 April. Available: https://twitter.com/ChuckTingle/status/1516952046942916608 (Accessed 22 April 2022).

Tomlinson, E. (2021) *Appropriation and Opportunism*. Available: www.project.credit/media/pages/journal/opportunism-and-appropriation-in-the-art-world/1582010369-1612385132/appropriation-and-opportunism-a-study-of-four-non-commercial-london-art-spaces.pdf (Accessed 3 March 2021).

Towers Open Fire (1963). Directed by Antony Balch. *The Final Academy Documents* [DVD, CRDVD13]. London: Cherry Red Films. 2002.

Valentine, J. (2004) 'Aesthetic Autonomy, Organisational Mediation and Contextualising Practices' in Harris, J. (ed.) *Art, Money, Parties.* Liverpool: Liverpool University, pp. 187–214.

Walsh, M. (2021) 'Remoter Viewing', *Art Monthly*, October. pp. 8–11.

Ward, C. (2004) *Anarchism.* Oxford: Oxford University.

Warne Thomas, C. (2021) *Artists as Workers.* Autonomy. Available: https://autonomy.work/portfolio/artistsasworkers/ (Accessed 12 December 2022).

Watson, J. (2009) *Guattari's Diagrammatic Thought.* London: Continuum.

The Wicker Man (1973). Directed by Robin Hardy. [Blu-ray, VFC97521]. Paris: Studiocanal. 2015.

Winkleman, E. (2009) *How to Start and Run a Commercial Art Gallery.* New York: Allworth.

Ziherl, V. (2016) 'In Search of a Flashlight: The Intimate Politics of the Curatorial' in O'Neill, P., Wilson, M. and Steeds, L. (eds.) *The Curatorial Conundrum.* Cambridge: MIT, pp. 217–25.

Index

For Product Safety Concerns and Information please contact our EU
representative GPSR@taylorandfrancis.com
Taylor & Francis Verlag GmbH, Kaufingerstraße 24, 80331 München, Germany

www.ingramcontent.com/pod-product-compliance
Lightning Source LLC
Chambersburg PA
CBHW060855170526
45158CB00001B/369